Dare to Rise

A Collection of Courage from
Eight Remarkable Women

©2024 Dare to Rise
a publication of Business in Heels International Pty Ltd

All rights reserved.

No portion of this book may be reproduced, stored in a retrieval system, or transmitted in any form or by any means – electronic, mechanical, photocopy, recording or scanning, or other – except for brief quotations in critical reviews or articles without prior permission of the authors and Business in Heels International Pty Ltd.

All rights reserved with the authors ©Business in Heels International Pty Ltd co-authors:

Anthea Enterkin
Terri Wilby
Mary Rose Chambers
Deb Fribbins
Philippa Rickards
Baishakhi Connor
Judith Jordan
Stephanie Lee

For further information and any questions visit our
Website www.businessinheels.com
Email info@businessinheels.com

ISBN: 978-0-6451639-5-7 (paperback)

Edited by Steve Sweeney

Compiled, produced, and published by
Business in Heels International Pty Ltd

Contents

Foreword by Amanda Campbell — 07

Anthea Enterkin — 11
   From bars to breathe — 13

Terri Wilby — 19
   A Breath of Life: A memoir of resilience — 21
   and transformation

Mary Rose Chambers — 31
   Monsters! monsters, everywhere.. — 33

Deb Fribbins — 43
   Making the right choices — 46

Philippa Rickards — 57
   The Marathon Within: A Journey of — 59
   transformation

Baishakhi Connor — 69
   Love, loss and new beginnings — 71

Judith Jordan — 82
   Kintsugi. A repurposed life — 84

Stephanie Lee — 95
   Embracing change in a new city — 97

Foreword by
Amanda Campbell

Life's journey is an unpredictable tapestry woven with threads of triumph and trial, joy and sorrow. Each thread tells a story of resilience and bravery, stitching together a narrative that is as unique as it is universal. Within this intricate design, we find the essence of human strength and the capacity to rise beyond our circumstances. As a Sports Kinesiologist and author specialising in Multiple Sclerosis and autoimmune diseases, my story has been one of profound transformation, making it an honour to pen the foreword for "Dare to Rise: A Collection of Courage from Eight Remarkable Women."

At the age of 24, I was thrust into a world of uncertainty with a diagnosis of Multiple Sclerosis. The physical and emotional upheaval was overwhelming. It wasn't just the disease; it was the fear of what lay ahead, the changes to my body, and the limitations that now seemed insurmountable.

By 29, I faced left-hand side paralysis, which was another blow to my already fragile sense of self. Yet, amidst the chaos, I discovered something extraordinary: the power of flexibility. Flexibility not only in my physical being but also in my mindset.

Through my journey, I learned that true healing begins in the mind. My experiences led me to develop a philosophy I now share through my book and work as a Kinesiologist at Bend Like Bamboo. Here, we focus on overcoming stress and limiting beliefs, optimising healing, and reducing autoimmune disease symptoms. I have seen firsthand how a flexible mindset transforms the ability to adapt, heal, and perform. It is this belief that has become the cornerstone of my mission: to help others re-imagine possibilities in their lives and bodies, finding strength in the face of adversity.

"Dare to Rise" embodies the spirit of this philosophy. This collection of stories is a testament to the indomitable courage that lies within each of us. Each narrative is a beacon of hope, a reminder that no matter how daunting the challenges, we have the power to rise. The titles in this collection—ranging from "Love, Loss and New Beginnings" to "Monsters! Monsters, Everywhere"—offer a rich tapestry of experiences that resonate on a deeply personal level. These stories illuminate the path from struggle to strength, providing a guidepost for those navigating their trials.

The essence of this book lies in its ability to show that courage is not the absence of fear but the willingness to confront it. The remarkable women featured within these pages have faced their own monsters and emerged victorious. Their stories serve as both a mirror and a map: a mirror reflecting our own struggles and a map guiding us toward our own resilience.

As someone who has worked extensively with individuals facing stress, burnout, and autoimmune diseases, I understand the profound impact that shared stories can have. They offer validation, insight, and inspiration. By learning from the experiences of others, we can gain valuable perspectives that empower us to confront our own challenges with renewed vigour.

This collection is not just a series of individual tales; it is a collective narrative of resilience, a testament to the strength of the human spirit.

The journey of healing—whether physical, emotional, or both—is deeply personal. Yet, as we explore the stories within "Dare to Rise," we realise that we are not alone.

The courage and strength depicted in these pages remind us that our struggles are part of a larger human experience. They offer solace and encouragement, helping us to understand that our pain can be transformed into power, and our setbacks into stepping stones. In my roles as a coach and keynote speaker, I emphasise the importance of uncovering blind spots and embracing the full spectrum of our potential. The stories in this collection echo this message, demonstrating that we open ourselves to profound growth and transformation by embracing our vulnerabilities and challenges.

As you turn the pages of "Dare to Rise," may you find not only inspiration but also a renewed sense of possibility. These stories are a celebration of the remarkable strength within us all. They are a reminder that no matter how formidable the obstacles, we have the power to rise, adapt, and flourish.

In closing, I am honoured to be part of this incredible journey. Let the courage of these eight remarkable women inspire you to embrace your own story with grace and resilience. Remember, as the Bend Like Bamboo philosophy teaches us, flexibility builds resilience, and resilience nurtures our capacity to heal and thrive.

Welcome to a collection that dares to rise.
May the force be with you,

Amanda Campbell

Kinesiologist, Author, Speaker
Founder of Bend Like Bamboo.

"Each inhale a reminder of life's transient beauty, each exhale a release of pent-up anguish and regret."

Anthea Enterkin

Anthea Enterkin's life illustrates resilience and personal transformation through her journey to becoming a breathwork practitioner and coach. Now living in Geelong with her partner and pets at age 67, her path has been marked by significant challenges. After high school and university, Anthea faced a 27-year heroin addiction, resulting in six years of prison in the 1990s.

Breathwork played a pivotal role in her recovery, enabling her to reconnect with herself and return home to help her Mother care for her Father who was suffering from Parkinson's disease and dementia. Her caregiving deepened bonds with her mother, healing past wounds and when her father died her mother asked her to stay on with her.

ABOUT THE AUTHOR

During those years with, her mothers support and encouragement. Anthea came off Methodone, commonly called liquid handcuffs. This enabled Anthea to live a full and unrestricted life and is and has been an encouragement to those struggling with their addictions that there is hope and it can be done.

The sudden death of her mother from pancreatic cancer was a turning point, inspiring Anthea to channel her resilience into personal growth. Breathwork continued to be a cornerstone of her transformation, leading her to study with a renowned breathwork coach for six years and become a qualified practitioner. This practice not only allowed her to discover her true self but also became her tool to guide others facing struggles such as addiction, anxiety, and self-worth issues.

Anthea's impact has been profound; she mentors young people and teaches breathwork at a local community center. Through Breathe Anew Coaching, she leverages her life experiences and empathy to help clients on their journeys of self-discovery and healing. Her dedication to this modality and personal development has made a lasting impact on her community, exemplifying how overcoming adversity can lead to helping others transform their lives.

Website	breatheanewcoaching.com.au
Instagram	/antheaenterkin
Facebook	/ajenterkin
Linkedin	anthea-enterkin

by Anthea Enterkin

From bars to breathe...

My first conscious memory traces back to the bars of my cot, a baby surrounded by the cries and screams of others in the orphanage. Little did I know that a similar sense of captivity would weave through my life, unfolding into a tale of self-destruction, resilience and transformation.

That orphanage shaped my early years with many endless hours spent viewing the world through the bars of my cot. Those cold metal rods became my first companions, silent incarcerating witnesses to the unreachable chaos of my loveless world beyond.

In a heartbeat it all changed, and I became the daughter of a strict primary school headmaster. In this dynamic, I experienced a unique form of favouritism – the absence of it. While I longed for validation, a glimmer of recognition or a hint that I was more than just another student in his eyes, my father, driven by a noble intention to maintain impartiality, inadvertently overlooked the emotional turmoil festering within me. I never thought I was special to him, worthy. So, despite excelling academically to prove my merit and bring myself to his attention, I battled inner demons and spiralled into anorexia as a coping mechanism.

Additionally, I found solace in the hollow embrace of self-destruction as my body become a battleground for silent wars-without-winners against myself.

The pursuit of academic excellence led me to university, albeit not the path I initially envisioned. Struggling with aimlessness and a gnawing sense of inadequacy, I stumbled into the clutches of addiction, seeking refuge in the ephemeral bliss of chemical oblivion. Heroin became my silent companion, whispering sweet promises of escape amidst the chaos of my existence. Days blurred into nights, and nights into days, as the needle punctured the veil between reality and illusion. Rehab became a revolving door, each stint a temporary respite from the relentless grip of addiction. Yet, like a moth drawn to the flame, I found myself ensnared once more in its fiery embrace.

In order to fund my habit, I had turned to crime. Smallish stuff at first…stealing goods from large stores and then returning them for refunds and shoplifting where I was able to exchange the goods for drugs. Then as my habit grew I began to target the banks….stealing other people's id's, opening fake accounts and passing stolen cheques through them. I became quite "good" at this and my deception went on for many years…until I mistakenly entered a bank where I had already stolen from them and I was chased and caught. My first real dealings with the police. I had been bashed and bruised by some of the officers I encountered but there were also a few genuinely caring people. This, of course made me hate myself more because I knew there was some light and love inside me. I just couldn't access any of it….especially any self-love.

by Anthea Enterkin

The old cells under the Melbourne Magistrates Court were cold, wet and demoralizing.

I was in my 30's, weighed 40 kgs and walked with a walking stick because of an early hip replacement (I have since had 3 replacements). I felt broken and hopeless. I cried a fair bit. My 27-year heroin addiction meant I was often in some police cell somewhere. Lots of cages and lots of bars, and I knew if I didn't stop doing what I was doing….I would probably end up in prison. I tried hard to kick my habit, succeeding for a few months and then reoffending. It had become difficult to get money, so I lived on the streets as a prostitute and continued travelling further and further away to steal from new banks.

Of course, society is not going to put up with that behaviour for too long and I was sentenced to 6 years with a 10 month minimum. My first night in the jail cells was horrible. I could hear other prisoners shouting or screaming at the guards, water dripping and as there was not much of me, I shivered with the cold all night. I witnessed some truly violent acts, and I was scared of what prison life was going to do to me. Would I ever be able to change? Next morning we all stood in line to be counted and I was given a telegram. Ooh. I wonder who this is from I thought?

It was from the Parole Board and had 5 ominous words on it. 'Parole and Pre-Release Denied'! That was it. No explanation…no-one to talk to about it…nothing.

It wasn't until lengthy incarceration became my reality that I was forced to confront the demons lurking within.

by Anthea Enterkin

Behind bars once again, amidst the clangour of metal and the suffocating weight of solitude, I discovered the power of breathwork and meditation. In the stillness of confinement, I learned to quiet the cacophony of my mind and embrace the rhythm of my breath. Each inhale a reminder of life's transient beauty, each exhale a release of pent-up anguish and regret. Meditation became my refuge, a sanctuary amidst the chaos, where I could confront the shadows of my past and envision a glimmer of hope for the future.

Despite the intensity of my journey, I emerged from the crucible of incarceration with a newfound sense of purpose and resilience. Post-release, I embarked on a quest for belonging and self-worth, a journey fraught with uncertainty and self-doubt. Years of soul-searching and personal development courses paved the way for transformative growth, yet the spectre of addiction lingered like a shadow, threatening to engulf me once more in its abyss.

It was during this tumultuous period that I was introduced to heart-centred breathwork, a gentle yet profound practice that would forever alter the trajectory of my life. Guided by the wisdom of my breathwork mentor, I delved deep into the recesses of my heart, unearthing buried traumas and long-forgotten dreams. With each breath, I shed layers of self-doubt and fear, embracing the radiant light of my inner being.

Caring for my ailing parents amidst my own battles, I confronted the harsh reality of cancer. Despite setbacks, I refused to succumb to despair. Instead, I drew upon the wisdom of my heart and the guidance of my breathwork mentor.

by Anthea Enterkin

Through the haze of chemotherapy and radiation, I found solace in the rhythmic cadence of my breath, a reminder that enduring resilience is possible amidst the ravages of disease.

Meeting my life partner Terese and my breathwork mentor marked a turning point in my journey, leading me down a path of profound self-discovery and healing. Together, we embarked on a mission to share the transformative power of heart-centred breathwork with others, guiding them towards inner wisdom and emotional liberation. I learnt to let out my anger and sadness....appropriately, and was able to start loving myself again....warts and all!

Through breath and heart, I have found healing, purpose, and a deep connection to myself and the world around me. I am now a qualified breathwork practitioner, my addiction is well in the past and I can hold my head up and continue moving forward. My journey is a testament to the resilience of the human spirit, a reminder that even amidst the darkest of nights, there exists the promise of a new dawn.

"Through it all, I have found strength in connection — to people, to nature, to breath, and to the spiritual wisdom that ties us all together."

Hi my name is Terri. I have had a bit of an unusual life but rich in experience and Trauma. I was born in post WW2 Britain to parents who had served in the war and who lost family members and friends. They had their own terrors and PTSD..... they both worked which was unusual. We moved around a lot 1st around Britain then we came to Australia starting in a small country town in South Australia, moving then to an Indigenous settlement in the Simpson dessert then to Victoria but always moving.

From under 16 we had moved 6 times and I had been to 6 different primary schools and I had experienced a lot of bullying both emotional and physical.

I had also experienced other trauma and abuse growing up .

ABOUT THE AUTHOR

At 16 my Mum left and then Dad followed her a week later leaving me with the house mortgage to pay and bills and my 14 year old brother to look after.

I found some direction thru finding God or God finding me....
I trained as a scientist then found that unfulfilling then joined a monastery..at the age of 24.

Through that time I studied and became a qualified spiritual director. Thru the life of silence and learning to listen to the Hearts Wisdom, studying Spiritual Classics, the life of the Dessert Fathers and modern classics focusing on a Loving Compassionate non Violent God I changed. The person who left the Cloistered part of the Monastary was someone I liked much better than the one who first entered. I was happier and more balanced and was beginning to like who I was.

Over the years I have done many personal development courses and worked on growing as a better person.

When I discovered Breathwork I discovered a simple way that would heal the trauma in my life and connect me to my heart and to its wisdom and guidance.

Through my experience of Breathwork I wanted to help others rediscover their Inner passion and purpose and to discover their best life maybe just a breath away!

Website	breatheanewcoaching.com.au
Instagram	@feelgr8247
Facebook	/terese.wilby.9
Linkedin	/terese-wilby

A breathe of life:
A Memoir of Resilience and Transformation

It was 8am on the twelfth day of March, a beautiful spring day. The gardens and fields were adorned with daffodils, crocuses, and bluebells. A freezing wind blew across the Irish Sea onto Fleetwood and my Mum was not faring well. Eleven months earlier, she had lost a baby boy so when the signs of labour started, Mum was rushed to nearby Blackpool Hospital, which was equipped to handle fragile infants in a new humidicrib.

My Mum was being wheeled into the hospital, grasping Dad's hand, amid a chorus of "DON'T PUSH!" Mum, of course, didn't want to push. My heart rate wasn't great, and she was growing tired and unwell. The doctors, prepared by the tragedy of losing Robert, were ready with the humidicrib and breathing tubes and I was delivered via emergency caesarean. 65 years later, I am writing this tale.

I grew up amidst the lingering trauma of two world wars, a global scourge that touched every nation and aged its people prematurely. Baby Boomers and our parents, who fought and toiled to create a safer world, now faced immense challenges. Many left their homes with just a couple of suitcases, seeking new opportunities away from the restrictive British class system.

by Terri Wilby

In my early years, when I expressed a desire to become a doctor, I was bluntly told, "People of your class can't go to Grammar school. Stick to secretarial jobs or sales."

My parents were part of the wave of migration that sought to escape oppression and seek a better future. As a toddler, I was perplexed by the cruelty and meanness of people. By age two in nursery school, I was already being held accountable for the actions of older kids because I was seen as being more mature and a peacemaker. Yes, this painful, lifelong pattern of struggling with injustice and cruelty began early on.

My early years were marked by a blend of wonder and fear. Aged two, I often ran to the end of the road, escaping my abusive babysitter, to find solace from the strong wind off the Irish Sea. The roar of the waves hitting the shore comforted me. There, I waited and listened for the rhythmic clip-clop of the beach donkeys' hooves. You see, The Donkey Man would lift me onto Neddy, my favourite, providing me a fleeting sense of security, as he led his herd to their stable to rest for the evening. After helping, the Donkey Man walked me back to the end of the street and I snuck back into the babysitter's house until one of my parents came to pick me up.

I was a sickly child with multiple allergies and a lung dysfunction. This meant many trips to specialists in London.

On one of these trips, Mum noticed a pub, the Black Swan. It was right next to Australia House. She would often be in there looking around, reading and talking to the staff about emigrating.

by Terri Wilby

By the time she had decided that's what we should be doing, she had already teed up a sponsored job in a place called Naracoorte that came with a house and a high position for Mum. At the time, Dad was a police detective but there were no police jobs on offer in the new country. Regardless, Australia... here we come!

So, in 1968, Naracoorte, a town of 900 people who did not like the English, nor other migrants, became our hometown. Mum was unhappy and when she saw a job for a matron in Kingston, 3 hours away, she took it. Dad ended up losing the job he originally found and then took any job that came up. He showed me resilience and the capacity to have a go at anything and work out how to do it. We rarely saw Mum. We heard that she had applied to the South Australian Government for a job as a Nursing Sister to care for 3 indigenous communities plus the people living and working on properties. Everard Park and Rowena Downs are the ones I remember. The Community she would be based at was Indulkana. Dad followed up with the government and saw they were looking for a storekeeper, so he applied and was accepted for that job and we ended up going there as a family.

Pre-war, Dad had been in the merchant navy and had been around the coast of Australia and around the world many times.

During the war, he had been in Special Services and had worked in every theatre of war, behind enemy lines and in enemy waters. Mum was a radio operator and code breaker for the Airforce and other services.

by Terri Wilby

Mum, probably more so than Dad, had always wanted to leave Britain and find freedom. She wanted a chance to be something important. She always felt judged and never good enough.

Both Mum and Dad felt that coming to Australia would give Rory (my brother) and I the opportunity to get degrees and have a better life than we would have in class-based UK.
I believe their spirit is the reason they were up for the experience of seeing parts of Australia few others had ever seen. They certainly made everything seem to us like an adventure. We had always been on the move in the UK and that was also the case in Oz.

The journey to Indulkana took 10 days. We traveled through small outback towns and the Woomera rocket base. (As Mum and Dad were working for the Government we could stay overnight!) It was both scary and exciting. The countryside was totally alien from the UK.

Yet, in some sense, I connected with the desert and the wide-open spaces as I did to the vast expanse of the Irish Sea. I loved the blowing dessert winds as much as the gusts from the Irish Sea. I loved the sense of freedom that came from big spaces that were empty of man-made structures. I would ride my "deadly treadly" (my bicycle) to high spots of ground, feel a bond with the land and breathe in the vast, open spaces, just as I had been able to breathe in the ozone and oxygen from the sea.

Rory and I watched mobs of kangaroos, emus and brumbies as they ran or grazed on what little vegetation there was.

by Terri Wilby

At 8 and 10 respectively, these scenes transformed us.
We loved our friendships with the Indigenous kids, and, as a family, we were invited to corroborees the other white people weren't allowed to attend. We felt accepted as a family and cared for. Probably for all of us, this was a first in our lives.
It is a place I want to go back to. It has been called the "dead centre". For me, I felt a sense of belonging with the land and all its life forms. I still do. It was amazing just being able to breathe. There is an energy and life that is both deep and ancient. There was time to ponder creation and Creator.
All four of us loved it.

A couple of years later, the superintendent said to Dad that Rory and I were going to boarding school and that Mum was heading to another job in Heidelberg, Victoria.
Once again, Mum did her thing and she and Dad quickly scrambled around to get things organised… job, housing and moving.

So Victoria… here we come!

At different schools, Rory and I bonded more with other migrants as we all faced bullying for our differences. When Rory was being bullied, his friends would come and get me to protect him. Throughout my life, people often came to me, sharing their burdens. Despite having few close friends, I became a confidante for many. I loved helping others navigate life, leading me to pursue various healing practices.

One day, out of the blue, Mum said she was leaving because she couldn't cope with Dad hitting me all the time. That night, she packed her stuff and left.

by Terri Wilby

The next week, Dad came to me with the mortgage book and bills and told me, now that I was 16, I was old enough to look after my brother and take care of the mortgage as it was going to be an asset for Rory and I anyway. Then he was gone. I found ways to create jobs, earn money, pay the mortgage, pay bills, look after Rory and for us to keep up with our schooling. I was forced to drop judo and playing the violin.

Around this time, I was invited to a Christian group and connected with something that fitted with my experiences with the sea and the centre of Australia. I became involved in leading youth and church groups. I went to La Trobe University and studied Biological Science and, with no jobs in the field, continued studying Medical Laboratory Science at RMIT.

Eventually, I became a Clinical Biochemist and worked at Royal Melbourne Hospital. All the time, I was searching Christianity, looking for the Being who embodied compassion and unconditional love, not the judgement I perpetually felt as a gay woman.

This journey led me to places where prayer was more about silence and learning to connect with the life transforming Being called Yahweh (Literally Breath) in the Hebrew scriptures. While biochemistry was my living, spiritual searching, seeking and sharing were my passions. Consequently, I continually had people coming and talking to me about their troubles.

During this time, I connected with a group of "monks" who spoke about the spiritual life as a journey. To them, baptism was a transformative process which takes us from the image of God during life to becoming like God… compassionate, loving and forgiving.

by Terri Wilby

So empowered by this was I that I left my job and moved to Geelong to check out their Monastery. I lived there for over 30 years until…

In 2008, my brother's sudden death shattered my world.

When he had been left in my care decades earlier, he had become more like my son than my brother. He was a judo champion, worked in the health department and had made a big difference in groups and individual's lives. His passing hit me hard. Then I discovered I was his executor and responsible for supporting my niece, Nakita, through this time.

Additionally, I was the only one left in Australia to look after Dad, who was frail and ageing. Rory had been helping him with jobs around the house… but, of course, not anymore.

I was conflicted. In the monastery, I was unable to be there for Dad or Nakita if they needed me. Yet, I loved the framework those routines and practices gave me.

I prayed and sought guidance.

I started having dreams where I was being guided away into another community where people needed me. I thought about all the folk who were in the monastery and how they were all there to help but there was only me to help Dad. I was the only relative on my brother's side to be there for Nakita if she needed me. Going through all these considerations, I decided to leave the monastery. Now, aged 50, I was out in the world confronting new challenges while caring for Dad and being there for Nakita.

by Terri Wilby

During this time, I rekindled some old friendships, particularly with Anthea, who was undergoing cancer treatment. Moving in to support her, our bond grew strong, rooted in shared spirituality and compassion. I cared for her through surgeries and chemotherapy and other grueling treatments. I looked for ways to improve her health so learned reiki and reflexology. During this time, while still caring for Dad, we found ourselves being the centre around which some young folk gathered. We shared life together and numbers grew. We still have connections with those amazing young adults. Some of them calling us the Grannies. Dad was amazing in how he listened and shared his wisdom and knowledge. He loved the connection he had with them. They came to his funeral and some spoke of their memories with him.

Over time, Anthea and I attended gatherings about how to create an income or start a business. We learnt about renovating and flipping property and at one of these events we heard about a retreat called Passionately Alive. This was described as the missing link between knowledge of how to create a business and how to uncover and clear the blocks that stopped that happening. After everything we had been through, we felt we needed to go. Passionately Alive deepened my understanding and started the process of healing my psychological trauma. Through heart-centered breathwork, I reconnected with my soul via wisdom and peace. This gave me the same feelings as when I stood in front of the Irish Sea and on the rocky outcrops of Indulkana.

When Anthea and I encountered additional financial and life challenges, we continued seeking growth and healing.

by Terri Wilby

Moving through life, guided by breath and wisdom, I sought answers about God and spirituality, leading me to various paths and places. At every juncture, I found solace in simple acts like breathing, connecting with the essence of the earth, and helping others.

Today, at 65, I am planning to live fully to 105, embracing life's journey with new vigour. I have lived a life marked by transformation, from facing early injustices to navigating the complexities of adulthood and caregiving. Through it all, I have found strength in connection — to people, to nature, to breath, and to the spiritual wisdom that ties us all together. Life's journey is still unfolding. It's filled with endless possibilities and deep connections. And thus, the journey continues, as I share my story, grounded in the resilience of love, breath, and being part of this magnificent planet.

"remember, my girl, no-one is indispensable!" I knew then that I would never let his life be wasted. I would turn his teachings into life lessons.

Mary Rose
Chambers

Mary Rose Chambers, an Office Manager and Workplace Happiness Specialist whose journey to becoming a Happiness & Mindfulness Coach & Workplace Happiness Specialist is as diverse as her own multicultural heritage. Having grown up, and studied, in the United Arab Emirates, she brings a unique perspective and a rich array of experiences to her work.

Amidst a world filled with stress and doubt, Mary shines as a symbol of optimism. Her journey serves as a powerful reminder that even in the toughest times, we possess the ability to reinvent ourselves and motivate those around us. Beyond her role as an Office Manager, she champions happiness, mentors mindfulness, and specializes in creating a workplace filled with joy and positivity.

ABOUT THE AUTHOR

Mary says "I'm a firm believer in taking chances, especially when your well-being depends on it. I love challenge. I love adventure. I love people. I love life. I'm a mum, a daughter, a sister, an aunt, a cousin, an employee, a business owner, a coach, a healer AND most of all, I am unique."

Website	magicalmary.net
Instagram	@angelic_mary
Facebook	/mary.r.chambers
LinkedIn	/mary-rose-chambers

by Mary Rose Chambers

Monsters! monsters, everywhere..

I've always been the backbone in the office, always been "that person" working silently in the background ensuring everything runs like a well-oiled machine. One of my previous managers constantly, and confidently, introduced me as "part of the furniture" and in my mind's eye, I tried to imagine, was I a desk? A filing cabinet? A server rack? An ergonomic chair that made the working hours comfortable? It made me laugh, until it didn't. Until I felt like I had lost semblance to a person, but now appeared to be an inanimate object that functioned as part of the office. It was that moment in the relationship when your ego tells you you're investing way more than you are withdrawing, and the scales are no longer tipped in your favor..

From the vast experience under my belt, I became adept at identifying two ugly monsters that lurked within us, and which wreaked havoc wherever they found shelter, and in time, I became adept at luring out the monsters and sometimes being able to defeat them with my secret weapons.

As with every knight in shining armour whose life began as a farmhand or a helper, I too, started my career in similarly humble beginnings.

by Mary Rose Chambers

My career began in the hotel industry where I mastered the art of being a server; the greatest strength in the industry being the ability to "people-please".

My circumstances caused me to shift gears and join the more rigid, corporate world of banking and finance. My debut in this new landscape was temporary in nature; I was on a 3-day contract to provide support to a newly formed team within a bank. Those 3 days grew to 6 years and propelled me into a career that I absolutely cherished, one that opened a whole new chapter in my life and helped me grow in ways I could not have imagined.

In my adolescence, I'd learned much of my work ethic from my father. He'd dedicated his entire life to just one employer. He grew from a yard-hand to a Regional Warehouse Manager for a large, multinational oil company based in the Arabian Gulf. This company took care of our living expenses during the entire length of my dad's tenure with them. He always expressed his gratitude to them for relieving him of the financial burden of our livelihood. The only "sacrifice" he offered was to work away from home all year. Dad moved every time they set up a new drilling site. He worked 3 months on and 2 weeks off, we saw him for a total of 8 weeks in a year. It was barely enough time for us to build a relationship with him BUT we all knew how very much he loved us and the sacrifices he made to give us the life he thought we deserved. I was number six out of seven siblings and the only one who dared to be different, the one who dared to question everything, the one who dared to break the rules and the ONLY one who got a walloping from dad more than once.

by Mary Rose Chambers

You see, he was a gentle giant who didn't believe in violence of any kind, never raising his hands or his voice, until I came along and challenged his patience and calm. I was also the only one who really talked with him. I asked him about everything. I remember asking if he had a retirement plan, and would he build a consultancy firm to give him purpose after he left his 9-5 job. He said he didn't want to do that because he was never going to retire. I questioned him about the decades of knowledge and skills he'd acquired, he just laughed and told me I needn't worry, and that he would always be able to use it because, "This company will let me work until the day I die." Sadly, he was given a forced retirement at the ripe age of 71, that's 6 years beyond the widely accepted retirement age of 65. He was still the strong, intelligent, and courteous, gentle giant I always knew as my dad, but the day he left his warehouse for the very last time was the day he gave up on life. I remember the look of bewilderment and betrayal on his face as he entered the house, it was as if he were a stranger in his own home. We were eager to celebrate his new freedom, but he saw it as an end to his usefulness. Barely a couple of months later, he became paralyzed from the neck down and, after spending 11 months in a hospital bed, he breathed his last. The doctors and nurses who treated him told us what an amazing patient he was despite being paralyzed.

They shared how he would teach others patience, how knowing he was about what was going on around him, and how much he loved each one of us.

It was from his hospital bed that he gave me one of his final lessons in life, it summed up the deepest hurt he felt, he said "remember, my girl, no-one is indispensable!"

by Mary Rose Chambers

Losing my dad so unexpectedly taught me about one of the monsters I needed to guard against, I hinted at half of this monster in the opening page of this story, but it wasn't until years later when I was fully able to understand who and what that monster was. It was a double-headed ogre; each head had a name that wreaked its own havoc. The monster was Ego & Fear. My father never studied beyond secondary school, he worked his way up the career ladder through hard work and dedication. His motivator - his growing family at home. As he progressed, he saw new, younger people joining the workforce, all holding a degree of some sort under their belt. He thought if he ever "asked" for something he rightly deserved he could potentially be replaced quickly by one of these new contenders. Fear was working its way through his psyche. Simultaneously, Ego would not let him dare to ask for fear of being rejected by his manager. WOW!! Do you see the stealth and trickery of Fear & Ego? Do you see how they weave their weapons against their victims to the point where the person feels trapped between wanting more for themselves, knowing there's better out there and yet being afraid to ask for fear of rejection in more ways than one? That is one monster no-one likes to face. The monster won the battle; it kept my father humble and trapped ALL his life.

Today, I lead a comfortable life, living up to the responsibilities of motherhood and womanhood. The infamous pandemic of 2019-2020 gave me the golden opportunity to become a certified mindfulness coach, and later I added the additional certification of Workplace Happiness Specialist to my accreditation. It became clear the "pandemic" was causing fear and havoc among people globally. We were forced to wear masks and sanitize our hands constantly.

by Mary Rose Chambers

We were forced to vaccinate ourselves against this terrible disease. We were kept in lock-down unclear about what was taking place behind the closed doors of politics. I wish I'd been more tech savvy at the time and made notes of what was happening. I had an awareness this pandemic was not what they said it was, instead I believed it was "a catalyst for change" and truly caring corporations would seize the opportunity to rebuild something better.

I had a lot of "a-ha" moments during the months and years that followed the pandemic. I discovered that I'd walked too closely in my father's career footsteps and was equally afraid to ask for what I deserved despite knowing that "more" was possible. I was too proud to have my ego bashed if my requests were denied. Too afraid to risk losing it all to someone younger, prettier, more talented, and better presented than I. I'd fed the same monsters of Fear and Ego. It was in a moment of solitude when I'd decided to focus on myself and build myself up again, (I'd been to hell and back a few times by then), I discovered there was more out there for me AND I deserved it. I worked hard and I didn't have to "prove" anything to receive what was justifiably mine.

Finally, I built up the courage to face the monster. I pushed myself. I motivated and prompted myself daily to "know" that I could do this. Then the moment came to ask for all that I deserved and… it was received with no resistance.

It took me by surprise and made me wonder why I'd not done it sooner. I could have had all this ease so much earlier in my career.

I then fully embraced my role as a Workplace Happiness Specialist. As part of one of my workshops to highlight the speed at which change can happen, I posed a challenge to the participants to call someone they'd not spoken to in a long time. A week later, during the review session, one participant shared that he had called his sister whom he hadn't spoken to for decades. He said the call went smoothly and at the end they both realized they couldn't recall the reason they hadn't spoken for so long. They had missed out on a lifetime of growth, family celebrations, change and love, simply because their Egos got in the way. Neither could remember the reason for the disconnect and neither was willing to risk humiliation and embarrassment by making the first move just to reconnect. Can you imagine the depth of loss of that time spent apart?

Another encounter with this horrid monster was owed to an interesting trait I'd inherited from my mother. Mum performed her duties as a wife and mother well, a little too well, in fact. She always put herself last and everyone and everything else first. In the beginning it was my son, parents, and job that I'd put before myself. After I married, I then had my husband, two more children, work colleagues and friends that I added to the list. After losing my parents I started to fill my life with other things like fostering rescue dogs and ended up rescuing some cats as well. My home became a modern-day Noah's Ark, filled with more people and animals that needed rescuing. I gradually developed a persistent cough. Initially it was diagnosed as silent reflux resulting from an earlier operation to remove my gallbladder. It was treated as such, but it became even more persistent and often left me breathless. One morning as I was driving with my daughter, it became so difficult for me to breathe that I wasn't sure we'd make it home.

by Mary Rose Chambers

I kept telling my daughter I knew I was breathing but I felt nothing from that breath. It felt like I was dying. I barely managed to park the car and had to call for an ambulance to help me, I was sure I was dying. After an entire day in emergency I was admitted to the hospital, my body was not getting enough oxygen. I literally was dying from asthma that I'd unknowingly developed. I'd been working extra hard and inadvertently put my own health at risk. Did you decipher what monster this was? Are you familiar with this one? Her name is "neglect" and she's a sneaky little "B". She's so silent, so subtle and so unassuming that you hardly notice her attaching herself like the parasite that she is. She grows exponentially, eating away at your self-worth and your self-pride, knowing you won't stop her because she's gorgeously disguised as sweet, helpful, nurturing, caring, reliable and relentless. You're unaware that she stole your values and demolished ALL your personal boundaries.

As I lay in that hospital bed, really breathing for the first time in months, it dawned on me just how much of myself Neglect had stolen. I'd given of myself to so many people and lost all boundaries. I even stopped caring for my own health. I made excuses for why I couldn't do things I loved and so wanted to do for myself. I'd given up on my fitness, healthy eating, physical appearance, and so much more. Every suggestion directed at helping me, was met with an "I can't because:

- of my work
- I don't have the time.
- I'm too tired when I get home.
- I don't have the budget for it.
- I'm too heavy to do that.
- I get dizzy if I don't eat as soon as I wake up" (related to intermittent fasting)

by Mary Rose Chambers

There were ready reasons (excuses) why I couldn't help myself. Had someone else asked for help, I'd have slayed every obstacle to get the job done.

Many a time "Fear" had stopped me in my tracks and kept me from achievements that would have definitely rendered a better version of myself. Fear of what people would say or think if I took some time for myself.

Growing up, we were not accustomed to having snacks and junk food. We were lean, healthy kids. As life got busier and more interesting, food equated to comfort. I learned to "hold on" to any hurt feelings, any failures, any hardships in my body, mostly my gut, which caused a lot of discomfort. My body grew and it became harder for me to shed the excess weight. Complications followed which required the removal of my gallbladder, making it even harder for me to digest certain foods and, therefore, harder to lose the unnecessary weight. Intermittent fasting had often been recommended and I always had the excuse that I felt dizzy and weak if I didn't feed my body as soon as I woke up. One fine day, tired of seeing my own unhealthy reflection, I decided to try fasting. Six kilos lighter, I discovered that I don't actually feel dizzy at all. In fact, the lighter I got, the better I felt. I'm now a raving fan and although I am not consistent, I do resume fasting as soon as I start getting heavier. Another interesting fact is that, since the age of around 9, I learned to fast during the Islamic holy month of Ramadan. This fast means one doesn't consume any food or drink (not even water) from dawn to dusk for a period of 30 days. When I finally decided to confront Ego and try intermittent fasting, I was reminded how easily I fasted during Ramadan (despite being raised a Christian) and that I need only apply myself to achieve this goal.

by Mary Rose Chambers

Monsters don't always hide under a bed or in a closet. They often lurk in the recesses of the mind.

Fear of anything hides deep within us; dormant until we confront it. Then it rears its ugly head and starts to wreak havoc with our mind and our body. We tremble, we stutter, we become nauseated and worst of all we lose faith in ourselves. Fear makes us fantastic in referencing past failures, hurt and pain. Fear is nothing but ego in disguise. Ego makes us shy away from every growth opportunity and Neglect turns us away from our human dignity.

If you're able to identify some monsters lurking in your life, look for the kryptonite that will destroy them. Often, it's self-love and self-worth.

"Whenever I start to feel sorry for myself, which I do from time to time, I think of others who have it far worse than I do yet are making the most of their lives."

Deb Fribbins

Deb Fribbins is an entrepreneur, speaker, mentor, coach, author, champion for equality and social enterprise advocate, her main focus has been, and always will be, to serve the community. She does this by working with startups, small businesses and the various charities in which she is heavily involved.

Deb has two great loves in her life. Her 2 sons who have grown to be strong, independent men who have forged their own careers. Two loving daughters in law and a grandmother of 2 delightful granddaughters with more to come. As her men are both, self-sufficient, her second love is that of serving the community both through DEB and her charities.

She has extensive knowledge, experience and expertise in coaching businesses to achieve their goals.

ABOUT THE AUTHOR

With over 30 years' experience as a National Buyer and Planner for Myer, David Jones, Target and Harris Scarfe, plus many small businesses across Victoria and Internationally. This breadth of experience has given her insight and understanding of her clients needs, reacting to their specific needs is paramount to the success she has achieved over the years. There is no one sure cure for all.

Her business skills have helped countless startups, small retailers, manufacturers and wholesalers. These skills are also applied to the numerous charities she takes great joy in supporting. Mentoring for the Small Business Mentoring Service (SBMS) has enabled her to keep a pulse on countless SME's throughout Victoria.

Make the right choices, in business and based on being RAD!
- Research the market of the specific business, event,
- Analyse the information thoroughly,
- DO IT, Take action based on the information at hand.

In the last few years results achieved utilising these principles have included:-
- A retailer who achieved a 48% increase in sales in just 2 months,
- A manufacturer who added $4million dollars to his gross profit though utilising new processes.
- A small business owner who made some staff changes that had a huge positive impact on the business and increased brand awareness and customer loyalty.
- A country store who added $100,000 to the business over the summer period.

ABOUT THE AUTHOR

My charity work is endless with a very active Rotary club who have become my family.

The Geelong Art Show has 3 key objectives.
- To support artists in Victoria to show and sell their artwork.
- To support Geelong and the surrounding community by showcasing the artwork.
- To provide all surplus funds to an Australian Charity.

I now make choices that are meaningful to me and have supported small business and the general public as much as I can.

Website	debexbiz.com
Instagram	@deb_5ds_to success
Facebook	/deb.fribbins
Linkedin	/deb-fribbins

Making the right choices

At age 18, I started to learn life was made up of choices! What I did not learn until many years later was to make choices for me. Eventually, I learnt making positive choices with a positive attitude would make all the difference.

I started my career in retail with the intent of it being a fill-in job until I started university. At that stage, I was following the path I thought I had always wanted… to become a teacher. When I had my interview with Myer, the HR manager, Mr MacDonald, saw something in me that I had not recognised, and he coaxed me to join the cadet training scheme. This was a well-organised training program which was recognised as the best in the country. Little did I know, the struggle to find my voice would eventually lead me to reframe my life and make my own choices.

This was the first time anyone had asked me what I wanted to do. Up to that point, my mother had made all the decisions on absolutely every element of my life. For the first time ever, I was asked to decide for myself. This led me to make the first choice that would guide my future life choices. I came home all excited as I had agreed, at the ripe old age of 18, to be brave and tell my parents I had made the decision that affected my life.

by Deb Fribbins

My mother was furious.

She immediately made an appointment with Mr. McDonald to interview Myer to see if she would allow me to work there. I cannot tell you how many trees were cut down to make wooden spoons to belt us for not doing exactly as we were told. This was the first time I got lectured but no beating. I made a choice and Mr McDonald was able to convince her it was right for me.

I got my first buying position in February 1975 as the buyer for the new Miss Shop Accessories. I was in seventh heaven. This was my escape as I was still being abused, physically and mentally, at home. At work, I could escape by burying myself in sales and trends and styles and my efforts rewarded with positive results. This was the first time in my life I felt worthy. At home, all I had to do was whatever I was told. At work, people did what I suggested. I learnt what being a part of a team meant.

Life was wonderful, compared to my first 22 years. Then in 1976, I made my second bold choice and married a man to get out of home. Mother thought he was wonderful, but a little short. (She had to find something wrong with him!) I felt strangely safe in this newly married environment as I was living as I always had. You see... in essence, I married my mother.

Whenever I start to feel sorry for myself, which I do from time to time, I think of others who have it far worse than I do yet are making the most of their lives. I have two friends who struggle with MS and all the complications it offers.

by Deb Fribbins

I have a sister who died too young after suffering breast cancer, followed by bone cancer then finally brain cancer. There are so many who are much worse off, physically, mentally and financially. My demons are issues caused through 50 years of constantly being told how worthless I am. To this day, my self-doubt still rears its ugly head. I have learnt to control this with my "Deb Lectures". I am grateful for the life I have had, the brain I can use, and wonderful experiences my choices have brought.

From a work perspective, I have constantly proven my worth by achieving and exceeding my targets. By burying myself in my work I could forget my personal life issues and look forward to coming back to work each day. It was the only place where I was not made to feel useless, worthless, ugly, loud, overbearing, overweight and obnoxious.

The married years got slightly better as I learned to succumb to the demands. As with my mother, it was easier to do whatever I was told rather than argue or suggest something I wanted to do. Long after I divorced, I realised the way to get what I wanted for me or my boys, was to ask for the opposite.

My husband travelled a lot. My friends told me later I was like Dr Jekyll and Mr Hyde because I was a completely different person when he was around. Eventually, I lost my circle of work friends because I was never able to socialise with them. I later realised I could not see them due to what may have been his inferiority complex. After all… "Any idiot could do my job."

In 1982, our first son was born. I had to resign from work as there was no maternity leave in those days.

by Deb Fribbins

In 1983, our second son arrived and the distance between my husband and I grew. I felt I could never tend to my children's or, God forbid, my own needs first. As my boys grew, they were receiving the same treatment as me. I tried to discuss positive reinforcement as a parenting method. However, this was not something that had been experienced so it fell on deaf ears. It was all about a good belting so they would not do it again. I knew this was wrong even though I had been bought up the same way. I knew I deserved to be beaten as I was such a useless person. However, I did not believe my 3- and 4-year-old children should go through life as I did. They have grown to be strong independent capable young men. I am so proud of who they have become and their attitudes to life and love.

I suggested we go to counselling. This was not deemed necessary as the issues were all mine. I just needed to understand what I was doing wrong. This is how I lived for the next 20 years. It took many years for me to understand it was not all my fault.

I have always buried myself in my business life and charity work. I have spent many years helping others, through my career, my charity work and my own business. I feel fortunate to have been able to support many trainees in the companies I worked for and see them blossom and exceed their expectations. My charity work through the years has always been supporting others. My current work is still with Rotary and the charity I started in 2022 which supports many other charities.

Exiting a domestic violence marriage was the third choice I made for myself and my boys. My mother told me to stay in the marriage. "You made your bed. You lie in it." She did not want the "embarrassment" of a divorced daughter.

by Deb Fribbins

According to her, I should stay and continue to be beaten to show what a wonderful mother she was. I invited my parents to my home one evening when I was bruised badly. I told them we were divorcing. Mother asked me what I did to provoke such a fight. "If I did not resist, he would get it over and done with quicker." I needed to protect my children, which she did not understand at all. My father never raised a hand to us, he was always there for support, although he never protected us from her. I often wondered why.

The Family Court ruled, and the boys and I were evicted. It seems the house was more important than the boys. Apparently, I still just needed to realise I was wrong and he was right. So suddenly, we had to find somewhere to live. We were given two weeks. Luckily for me, my parents were going on the big retirement holiday to Europe so we went to house sit for 3 months.

By the time the property settlement went though, I was finding my feet and becoming more protective of my boys. They did not deserve to miss out. I spoke to the real estate agent who got the house cleaned and tidy for open inspections and it soon sold for more than the asking price.

At that time, his custody rights with the children were: -
   Week 1 – Pick the boys up Friday after school and take back to school the following Monday.
   Week 2 – They were picked up from school Friday afternoon, to have them home to me by 9 pm that night.
   They went away for 8 weeks of school holidays every year.

I was always concerned about what was happening to them while away from me.

by Deb Fribbins

Each year on his birthday, his parents' birthdays, Fathers' Day etc. he made sure he had the boys and would swap weekends with me if necessary. When it was my birthday, or the boys, or my parents or Mothers' Day, I did not have the same entitlements with the boys and no swap could occur. Again, I felt the reinforcement of my worthlessness on any special occasion. Speaking to the lawyer I was advised not to swap when it suited him as I did not have a right to swap with him to suit my needs. I could not do that to my boys, they would grow up with a better attitude to family life.

I was asked to apply for a job at the Target Buying Office in Geelong. That was the next hardest decision I had to make in my life. Another Deb Lecture…

I would lose all my support structures and take the boys away from their father. I agonised long and hard and sought support from the boys' school principal who said take the job. Eventually, I spoke to my dad at length. I needed to get away from mum and my ex and all the negativity for the boys' sakes. Not to mention the physical and emotional turmoil I was living in. I believe this was the best decision of my life. We drove back to Adelaide about every 4 weeks. The boys went to their dad every Christmas holiday for 4 weeks plus two weeks in term breaks 1 and 3. I never stopped him from seeing or having them but I lived in fear of what might happen if they wronged him. There were several instances over the years where the boys came home most unhappy. I did not always get the answer, as they were sworn to secrecy over what they did during these times.

When Target introduced planners to the business, each buyer was allocated one to work through the financial side of the business. Planning was the easy part for me as maths was my forte.

by Deb Fribbins

I found it boring though and preferred the challenges of buying the right stock for the consumer. I was told I would head up the planning role in ladieswear with another woman. I was not given a choice. My needs and wants were irrelevant.

If you wanted to apply for a promotion or a job in another area you had to get permission from your current boss. An opportunity came up so I asked my boss at the time if I could apply for a role back in buying. He explained to me "as long as he had any say, I would never get back into a buying role." It was late on a Friday afternoon.

I cried all the way home in the car and most of the weekend. The boys were away on a scout camp so I had time to think and do what I had always done… I gave myself a "Deb Lecture". I looked at all the pros and cons and discussed each at length with myself.
I decided I had two choices. (It always came down to choices.) I could stay in the role I had and make the most of it, or I could start looking for alternative jobs, resign and move on. Just another choice in life.

I went through my TEARS process: -
   Thoughts about the issue and how to control them.
   Emotions evoked in me and my family, how helpful is it?
   Actions to achieve my goals.
   Relationships that will enhance my life goals.
   Success. It will reward myself and those near and dear to me.

I decided to start looking for a job outside Target. Was it time for a complete change? Something with less pressure, less hours, more work life balance, less travel?

by Deb Fribbins

On arriving at work Monday morning, I was called into the boss's office. He told me I had been appointed to the role I wanted to apply for, the previous Friday. I asked him why he put me through hell all weekend. He said he did not want to make it easy for me. I needed to appreciate the opportunity he was "giving me". It took me all my effort to not resign then and there out of spite. Who would lose then? Only me.

I worked in retail for more than 40 years with all male bosses, until the last. Each of them was excellent at gaslighting and controlling women in this male-dominated field. Being dominated felt quite normal for me.

My last year at Target was very difficult for many reasons because my final boss was my mother all over again. The only thing missing was the wooden spoon. I began to feel less worthy every day as I felt constantly belittled in front of others. I felt myself being treated as I had previously and fell back into old habits of being subservient and not being allowed to make any decisions. My health suffered at this time. After a short stay in hospital, followed by many specialist appointments, I used all my sick leave, annual leave and long service leave to regain my mental strength. On returning to work I asked for a change of department. Permission was denied. I was told to go back to the same abusive environment.

Another Deb Lecture. It was time to resign.

I started DEB, Developing Excellence in Business, to support small business owners to exceed their expectations and live the life they want for themselves. I am devoted to my clients and devise systems for each of them to suit their specific needs. The principles of management do not change, but the choices made need to be treated differently depending on the client and their clientele.

by Den Fribbins

I love what I do. I have finally become the teacher I wanted to be 40 years ago.

I have a motto... Be R.A.D.
    Research all factors of the situation.
    Analyse the information and the impact on those affected by it.
    DO IT your way and make it work.
In essence, this is my Deb Lecture method.

I get great joy from seeing my clients achieve and exceed the results they want through utilising the skill sets and systems we develop. Business is difficult, but there are ways to turn it around with the right choices.

One of my recommendations to all businesses is to have a strong sense of Corporate Social Responsibility (CSR). In this, I practice what I preach. Six like-minded friends and I started a not-for-profit, The Geelong Art Show, in 2022.

My life learnings, are very simple: -
- Be a passionate, determined, charitable person.
- Believe in yourself.
- Ignore the negative comments from others and look for a positive resolve.
- Look at the big picture, the vision, in every decision.
- What impact would it have on my life, my boy's lives and those near and dear to me?
- Be grateful for the learnings along the way.

I am grateful for these lessons. They have helped me towards a better life. I do not dwell on the past. I choose to ignore it, move on and not repeat mistakes.

by Deb Fribbins

Every occasion in my life needing choices is carefully analysed to make what I believe is the right choice for me and my loved ones and the ones I serve.

"Perfect? Failure? What do these words really mean? In the end, I decided they didn't mean anything to me. "

Philippa Rickards

Philippa Rickards is the vibrant and optimistic founder of My Bookkeeping Buddy, where she brings a unique blend of expertise, passion, and positivity to the world of bookkeeping. A devoted mum and proud nanna, Philippa places family at the heart of everything she does, believing that strong family bonds are the foundation of a fulfilling life. Despite living with several medical conditions, Philippa's glass-half-full attitude shines through in her work and personal life, allowing her to not only run a successful business but also make meaningful contributions to her community.

Philippa's life is a testament to her belief that challenges are opportunities in disguise. She has raised three daughters, a role she considers her greatest accomplishment, and continues to inspire others with her unwavering positivity.

ABOUT THE AUTHOR

Whether volunteering in her local community or enjoying a theatre performance, Philippa's love for life is evident in everything she does.

Her approach to bookkeeping is simple yet profound: to give her clients back their time and reduce their stress so they can focus on what truly matters to them. For Philippa, bookkeeping isn't just a job—it's a way to make a difference in the lives of others, and she loves every moment of it.

Website	mybookkeepingbuddy.com.au
Instagram	@philippajrickards	@mybookkeepingbuddy
Facebook	/philippa.rickards.1975	/mybookkeepingbuddy
Linkedin	/philippajrickards	/6597853

by Philippa Rickards

The marathon within: A journey of transformation

As I sit here today, years later, I still wonder…
Was I running towards something wonderful and miraculous, something hopeful and worthy of my efforts? Or was I running away from something because I feared the past would catch up to me? Was I blowing away the cobwebs or just burying the failure? Clarifying my thoughts or clouding my judgement? As I regularly pounded the pavement training for my half-marathon, the answers to these questions became less and less important. Being in motion was all that mattered. You see it's harder for memories to hit a moving target.

So, I kept training and kept moving and began to replay my life…

Problem child. Not good enough. Try harder. No matter what I did, no matter how hard I tried it was never enough. I was never enough, I had to be perfect, anything less was simply not acceptable. Why did I think this? Because I lived it every day.

I remember always being in trouble, always doing something wrong, never being good enough. I know my mum tried her best, I know she was working with what she had, but at the time it was tough.

by Philippa Rickards

Between six and ten, I was constantly taken to every therapist under the sun. I couldn't tell you whether they were psychiatrists or psychologists or what type of therapist they were, but my mother firmly believed that there was something wrong with me and I was the problem child. At the last therapist, she took me to, I remember doing a whole lot of tests and being asked an awful lot of questions and then sitting in a huge leather chair in front of a big old-fashioned desk and kind of listening. I was staring out the window at this tiny bird in a tree. He told my mum that there was nothing wrong with me and that I had an IQ higher than she was capable of dealing with.

You would think this would be a thing to celebrate. Instead, it was the beginning of a whole new chapter. It began the merry-go-round of private schools and scholarship applications and tests and having to be the best in the world at everything. I don't remember how many entrance exams I sat, but it was a lot. I was accepted into most of them and, finally, my parents selected one school, and I loved it.
It was tough being a scholarship kid in a private school. Carrying the expectations of my family was hard enough. More damaging was the fact that my siblings got into the school under the sibling acceptance policy, meaning if I lost my place, they lost theirs too.

I couldn't fail.

Academically, I had to be perfect. I sat every test or exam there was, entered every competition and the results mattered. It wasn't good enough to be top 1% of Victoria and top 5% of the country in Maths and Science... I had to be top 1% of Australia. I remember coming home and telling mum I got 99% on an end of year exam and she asked me, "What happened to the other 1%?"

I started there in year six and had to leave halfway through year ten. Unfortunately, the recession hit, and private school fees are expensive.

by Philippa Rickards

The local high school wasn't great, and my parents had high expectations so off I went to sit another entrance test for a select entry high school that also had a sibling policy. Of course, I was accepted and so were my sister and brother. This was tough though as again… I couldn't fail.

On top of school, Mum also believed in extracurricular activities, and I think I did something most days of the week after school and then netball competitions on Saturday. By year eleven I simply burnt out. I had Chronic Fatigue Syndrome, I was exhausted. It didn't matter though, I still needed to be perfect, failure was not on option.

So where is my dad in all of this? He was there, but he was under his own pressures. When I was younger, he worked in a job that took him overseas a lot, so before my siblings came along, I spent much time with nanna and granddad as mum would go too. That's just what they did in the 70's. He was always at work or if he was home, he was in his study…

That study was a wonderous place with shelves on every wall packed with folders and files and papers. Eventually there was a computer. It was a magical device; a rectangular box called a Macintosh with this box with buttons on it attached to a string that would move an arrow on the screen and a typewriter that also connected to the screen. You could even do maths and numbers in this program called MYOB and my world opened up in ways I could never imagine.

I think dad could see my potential and my love for all things numbers and business.

by Philippa Rickards

I learned our family business from the ground up. I started at around twelve-years-old and by the time I was fourteen, I could do most things. I could answer phones, serve customers, quote jobs, provide the orders to the factory, manage workloads, do the bookkeeping. In the school holidays, when dad's secretary wanted time off with her kids, I would cover her job. I had the respect of the staff in the business because they knew I could do the job, and I had earnt it.

This is where I found my passion, my love of all things business and the one thing that kept me going no matter what was to come. At fifteen or sixteen, I even went and helped a friend of my dad's in his business, to cover the administration role when his staff member went overseas. I was a kid in an adult world, but I was damn good at this. Funnily enough, I still didn't see it as being my career, my passion or my life's work at the time.

So here I am eighteen years old, having survived my childhood, graduated high school, got into university to start the career I thought I wanted, I had some great friends, but I was miserable. I had to escape (not that I knew that's what I was doing at the time). I couldn't stay at home anymore as my parents' marriage was deteriorating and my relationship with mum bordered on toxic.

Eventually, I got my own flat in a sketchy neighbourhood, but it was mine and for the first time I felt free. Life, however, had other plans as after a car accident followed by a broken ankle, I found myself living with my boyfriend and his mum and looking for a new career.

Fast forward 5 years and the boyfriend became the ex-husband, I had 2 daughters under 3 and I was still looking for a new career.

by Philippa Rickards

Mum told me I had made my bed and now I needed to lie in it. In her eyes, I was a failure... again.

Looking back at it now, I was running then, and I have always been running. My ex-husband is not a bad guy, we were just young and we are so much better now as friends than we were as husband and wife. We make a great team as parents and now grandparents and that's what really matters. I am so proud of the fact that we could put our own differences and issues aside for the benefit of our kids.

Then, however, I needed money. The fastest way to get work was a temp agency, so I typed up a resume and made the calls. I was registered with three agencies and the work came flooding in. Even if I was working for agency one on a job, they would call me and move me to another one that paid them more money. This was when I realised that I had very marketable skills. This was when I made the leap and changed my life...

Starting my bookkeeping business was scary. I needed to go back to school at night to get more training and needed to work around my kids. I did what I needed to do to give them everything they needed. Sometimes, though, I think they needed more of me. My business ensured I could be there for the concerts and special events, it allowed for the holidays we took and the house I built. It gave us a foundation to build a strong family that continues today.

Within 5 years, I had over 75 clients and 2 staff and things were great. I met my second husband, he joined the business, and we branched out into other areas.

by Philippa Rickards

The business went from strength to strength and even allowed for me to take time off to go through IVF to have another child. This was also a very tough process and luckily, we got our daughter on the last try because after nine miscarriages, I was done. Years earlier at 25 I had had a stroke, and it turned out I had a blood clotting disorder that also impacted on pregnancy. I was incredibly lucky to have had my older children also.

Turns out the world I had built for myself was constructed on sand and it all shifted in the blink of an eye. My husband had been hiding things and could no longer cope with his life. He had a complete nervous breakdown and ended up in a private psychiatric hospital for many months. I was now trying to support my husband, my 3 children, over 200 clients, 5 staff plus plus plus.

I got home one day and opened a letter that had been delivered and my legs went out from underneath me. My world as I knew it came crashing down and things had to change again. Turns out he had over $500,000 in debt that he had gone bankrupt on and most of it had my name on it. It was now my responsibility. I fought it for 3 years, I tried to prove I didn't sign anything, I tried to prove it wasn't my debt. I failed. On many occasions, I actually got on the floor under my desk and curled up in a ball and cried. The pressure was overwhelming and… I cracked.

It was a week after my 34th birthday and I decided I wasn't doing this anymore. I put my house and business on the market and decided it was time to move on. Selling the house I had worked so hard for and the business I loved evoked so many feelings of not being good enough, of being a fraud ("See I told you you couldn't do it!") of being a failure but I

by Philippa Rickards

ignored them, I pushed them down, I got busy, there were things to get done, I was running.

For the next two and a half years, I ran a micro bookkeeping business on the side, just a few clients that didn't want to be sold with the business plus I worked for a few accounting firms. A wonderful friend had initially made an introduction, and things went from there. Somehow, I just seemed to get headhunted to better and better roles and eventually I was working for a firm based in Sydney and I would travel a few times a month, but I got to work from home.

The best thing about this was that I could go for a run whenever I needed to. It had started when I was trying to get out from under the debt. When it got too much I would go for a walk. A walk turned into a run and a run turned into getting a coach and that turned into training to run the Melbourne Marathon. Just the half marathon to begin with. I had already done a 5km, then a 7.5km, then a 10km and finally a 12.5km. My times were good and my coach was happy. I was never going to come first but I just wanted to achieve that 21km and get over the line.

I also had my own clients in my micro bookkeeping business plus family and friends and my half marathon goal. For the first time in a long time, I was actually happy, I had made it, I was a success, and then my world crashed down again.

Things had been really busy, I had run the 12.5km race, then gone to Sydney for 3 days. I woke up one day feeling horribly nauseous. Four days later, I was in so much pain and so dehydrated my family took me to hospital.

by Philippa Rickards

Hours turned into days and days into weeks of hospitalisation and eventually I got the diagnosis of Crohn's disease. That's ok, I thought... just something else to add to the list of things I need to manage. Give me some medicine and I will get back to my life. I tried, but it turned out my body didn't get the memo. It decided that it would be a law unto itself.

I never did get back to work in my amazing dream job and I have not run a step since that 12.5km race. For over a year I tried mind-over-matter, but every time I did, I would end up back in hospital. I spent about 70% of my time in hospital that first year and about 50% of the second.

I had failed again.

My body decided to react badly to many of the medications and initially one of these reactions was not being able to breathe well, this meant I needed steroids, and the use of steroids led to developing diabetes. The medications to treat Crohn's disease lower your immunity and as such I was catching every virus and bug going around usually attacking my lungs and I had multiple bouts of pneumonia. Trying to manage multiple conditions where the medications are triggering each other is complex and over the years we just kept adding more and more problems. As it stands right now, I stopped counting at 10 medical conditions that need managing with over 20 medications.

In January 2020, my dad brought the papers to my hospital bed, and I signed the contract for my house in Geelong. I was moving there to be closer to my oldest daughter and granddaughter and for a new life. It was time I took control again and if I was never able to return to the work I was doing before I got sick and was lucky enough to get my super and a TPD payout then I needed to use it wisely.

by Philippa Rickards

I had spent the previous two and half years being a sick person and didn't want that to be my identity. I knew I had a long road ahead. I was not going to live in failure.

Then COVID hit the week we moved house, and I was so fearful that I would catch it and die that I was somewhat grateful for lockdowns as it made me feel safe. It also strengthened our family bond as my middle daughter stayed with my youngest daughter and I a lot plus my oldest daughter was pregnant again and had my second granddaughter, so we had a family bubble to support each other.

When the world opened again after COVID so did my life. I embraced my new community and through many business networks in Geelong I have made so many connections. I've never been good at making friends but even that is starting to happen. While the fears are still there, they are getting smaller. I am lowering the walls and letting people in. My bookkeeping business is thriving, and my health is slowly improving and while I will never get better, I am getting better at listening to what my body needs and reacting appropriately. I also allow myself to feel things instead of running from them.

Perfect? Failure? What do these words really mean? In the end, I decided they didn't mean anything to me. I did learn that pushing down my feelings, not dealing with my stress, just striving to keep going, is not the best way to live my life. It's probably why I got so sick in the first place.

I realised that I am a survivor and that I am incredible. The only opinion that matters now is my own. I have overcome domestic violence, nine miscarriages and 2 divorces.

by Philippa Rickards

I have lost everything and rebuilt my life from the ground up financially, emotionally and physically more times than I want to count and learnt what really matters. I have accepted that I am a disabled person and will have health challenges for the rest of my life, but this doesn't mean life can't be amazing. I have found self-worth, and I know my passion. I don't need to run anymore.

"I had learned to let go, to embrace life without trying to control every outcome."

Baishakhi Connor

When Baishakhi was 8, she dreamed of becoming the US President! Growing up in small-town India on a healthy dose of fiction, anything seemed possible. At 12, she realised a one-way flight to US cost many years of their household income! Presidency dreams shifted to chasing opportunities beyond her near-poverty-line status.

Baishakhi carved a diverse career spanning four continents. She cracked one of the world's most competitive exams and completed her MBA from India's most elite institution. She criss-crossed the globe as an investment banker advising global industry titans on multibillion-dollar mergers and acquisitions. She was engaged to the love of her life.
She had it all.
Until she didn't.

ABOUT THE AUTHOR

This is the story of the year that shattered Baishakhi's definition of success and pieced it back together into a more authentic reality. It's a story of love, loss, and new beginnings. It is why today Baishakhi introduces herself by far more than her corporate job.

Now in her 40s, Baishakhi stretches boundaries in ways she never imagined at 8. She serves on a Not-for-Profit Board, volunteers, mentors, speaks and writes regularly on LinkedIn addressing 28,000 followers. She makes time for new things, currently flexing her muscles into Powerlifting. She lives in a tri-cultural tri-religious family with her Australian Catholic husband and Afghan Muslim foster daughters. As foster mum of 2, stepmum of 4 and step grand-mum of 7, Baishakhi's life today is a busy blur of family, fun and food.

This story is the year that started it all.

Linkedin   /baishakhiconnor

Love, loss, and new beginnings

The morning after my honeymoon, I was laid off from my dream job. It was December 2008. It had taken 30 painstaking years to build up the success I had always dreamed of. And mere minutes for it to all come crashing down.

Up to that point, that year had been the best year of my life. I had just earned my MBA from one of the most prestigious, most select schools in India. I was living in bustling Hong Kong, working at one of the top investment banks of the world, advising titans of global industry on multibillion dollar mergers and acquisitions. I had criss-crossed the globe, living out of a suitcase the entire year, moving across Bengaluru, Mumbai, Kolkata, Hong Kong, London, Melbourne, Cairns.

I had it all, or so I thought.
I married the love of my life that year. Twice! Surrounded by our closest friends and family, we walked round the fire seven times in Kolkata. Said "I do" again in Melbourne. And jetted off to an idyllic island in the Great Barrier Reef for our honeymoon.

The morning after, even before I could walk to my desk, I got laid off. At 11 am I boarded one of the many convenient Hong Kong buses to get back to my apartment. The mid-morning sun cast an indifferent glow on the bustling streets.

by Baishakhi Connor

11am was meant for a bustling office, PowerPoints, Bloomberg terminals, DCF models, transaction multiples, football field charts... Instead, an endless expanse of blank canvas took up the sudden vacancy of my professional life. Familiar sights blurred past the window, yet my gaze remained fixed on the emptiness within. I wanted to feel the surge of anger, the flood of tears. None came. Instead, the thick fog of a hollow numbness muffled the world around me while I was adrift in a sea of nothingness.

In case you are feeling sorry for me, remember I worked in the financial world. The Bloomberg terminals told me every day what was happening. One of the many multibillion dollar acquisitions was that of my own employer by the Royal Bank of Scotland. I knew the top dollar paid for the acquisition had brought RBS to its knees. I knew colleagues who had jumped ship, warned me it was sinking. Right before I left to get married, everyone was bracing for a layoff announcement we all knew was coming. What's more, while on my honeymoon my best friend called. "I don't want you to be surprised when you get back. Your entire team has been dissolved. Everyone has been laid off."

Yet there I was. Still believing I was God's own gift to mankind. Still thinking I would of course remain the star I was.

"Never mind," said Geoff when he heard, his hand finding mine in a comforting gesture. His tone was reassuring, despite the uncertainty hanging in the air.

With a new look and newfound determination, I set off to tie loose ends in Hong Kong and prepare for the next chapter of my life.

by Baishakhi Connor

I organised my taxes. I transferred money to Australia. I gave notice to my landlord and for the very first time in my life, I bought a one-way ticket into an uncertain, unplanned, unknown future...

Suddenly, I was newly married, newly jobless, about to move house, move countries, and become a new immigrant.

Little did I know the tumultuous journey that lay ahead.
Geoff and I extended our honeymoon to make the most of my newfound "freedom". We went to magical Macau. Spent weeks on beautiful Queensland beaches. By the time we finally reached what was to be my new home in Melbourne, I was recharged, refreshed and ready for what I thought would be a quick job hunt into my new glamorous Australian job.

The house I moved into had been Geoff's for the previous two decades. It harboured memories. Walls held the weight of secrets shared. As I set about cleaning with gusto, I found forgotten Easter Eggs from hunts of years gone by. Once I found a note saying "Dad said Ricki-Lee Coulter will win this season" – from a happy 2004 evening with the kids watching Australian Idol.

Kids? Did I mention I was also a newly minted stepmother of four teenagers? Love does make one brave.

20 years ago, Geoff had built the house with another new wife, a little baby and dreams. They raised four children, lived through a marriage, a bitter divorce, and then he faced life as a single dad.

The house was full of voices. Human presence breaking the solitary existence I had been used to for 15 years.

by Baishakhi Connor

Objects shifted surreptitiously. The saltshaker I placed on the pantry shelf now lying crooked on the table. Dishes appeared in the sink when I had neither cooked nor eaten. The few trinkets from my past, once carefully arranged, remained hidden away in the wardrobe as I struggled to find my place in our home that once was just his.

By the end of January 2009, Australia sweltered through a 1-in-a-100-year heatwave. The scorching summer heat clung to my skin like a persistent reminder of the unfamiliarity of this new chapter. I threw myself into the job hunt with enormous enthusiasm. Each day began with the ritual of opening my laptop, the soft hum of the air conditioner a constant companion as I scrolled through job listings, carefully tailoring my resume and cover letter for each one.

Slowly, the hope morphed into a nagging dread. The silence grew louder with each passing week.

In February, 200 people perished in a bushfire near where we lived. Temperatures climbed to 43 degrees. I struggled to breathe the smoky dry stifling air. My nose bled often. I kept applying.

The first ever elected female prime minister in Australia was sworn into office in March. After herculean efforts, the bushfire was finally contained. I researched LinkedIn every day and reached out to strangers, asking for career advice over coffee. And kept looking.

The weather changed, trees turned golden and adorned streets below with autumn leaves.

by Baishakhi Connor

Faint echoes returned from my efforts. The Aussie twang felt less foreign. Arvo, footy and brekkie became less cryptic. The job remained elusive. The overcast skies mirrored my growing frustration as rejection emails trickled in, each one a blow to my confidence. "We regret to inform you..." became the soundtrack of my days, the polite rejections piling up in my inbox like fallen leaves in the gutters outside.

Employers I met helpfully told me how they only interview students from Melbourne or Monash Universities or students from a small selection of elite private schools. Every organization wanted local experience. The university name that would open any door in India now prompted a quizzical "Is it any good?" question. The years of international experience I was so proud of now felt like a useless, distant echo.

It took until April for the first fruits of labour to show. A few days before my birthday, I met with David, a brilliant recruiter who called me back as soon as I sent my resume. He had a risk management role with a private equity managed energy company. It was the sector I was covering a few months ago at the investment bank and a role that fit me perfectly. I met with their financial controller within days and had a superb interview... one of those where you just feel the connection. He organised a final interview with their partner who was arriving back from US the following week. It was all confirmed and I prepared extensively despite David telling me it was in the bag. This would simply be a conversation to close out the process, he said. I wasn't taking any chances.

The evening before my meeting with the partner, David called at 7pm. "There's been an interesting development," he said. "Believe it or not, they've decided to..." As he paused, I was ready to celebrate. Perhaps they decided to not go through another interview just for formality??

"… put the role on hold", David continued.
I slumped like a pierced balloon.

I looked at my prepared notes on risk metrics and the doodles of what I'd do when I have a job and the spending money I'd been missing which had kept my life on hold. Despair stared back at me from the notes.

I would not get another interview for 5 months.
Winter settled in, bringing with it a biting cold that seeped into my bones. The days were shorter, the nights longer, and my resilience was tested by the dark early evenings.

Geoff, in the meantime, had decided he would start a business. His optimism was a stark contrast to my own faltering confidence. On his birthday in February, he registered our new family business. For a few hours each day, I got off the hamster wheel of job applications and recharged by building a new website, setting up MYOB accounting, taking phone calls from clients, or placing ads in the local paper. Geoff went back to refresh his electrical license, with our firm conviction that an essential service would be more recession proof than other businesses. It would turn out to be a good decision.

In the dreary winter after my near win in the job market, we needed to make space for Geoff's expanding business machinery and vehicles. For a small home-based business, this meant we would build a brick driveway along the entire length of our backyard.

In true blue Aussie style, Geoff decided we would do this on our own! I had grown up on heavy doses of my mum warning me to "Study hard!

by Baishakhi Connor

Or you might end up a labourer laying bricks!!" That month, we made sure to send maa a photo of me laying bricks.

I introduced the family to their first Holi (festival of colours). The backyard and our new DIY brick driveway transformed into a canvas of chaos and laughter. The air filled with bursts of colour as we ambushed each other; no one safe from the playful attacks. At one point, they ganged up and cornered me, wide grins on their faces. Before I could react, they pounced, covering me in a cloud of green and yellow. I laughed so hard I could barely breathe. After the frenzy, we collapsed on the grass, our faces streaked with colours and tears of laughter. My heart expanded with a sense of belonging and love.

Geoff comes from a very large family, and I felt right at home in these gatherings. Our family birthdays often brought together over 100 close family and friends. His Maltese heritage meant there was an abundance of food which my Indian brain found familiar.

By September, I was exhausted. Something had to give. The job front was just as bleak. But spring brought a gradual thaw, both in weather and in spirit. I had been putting life on hold for too long, waiting for when I got a job. Finally, I gave in and we bought last-minute tickets to visit my family in India.

It was my biggest festival of the year – Durga Puja - and it was a privilege to show Geoff what a spectacle it was back home. Geoff and I visited my school. We also took the opportunity to travel with my family to neighbouring Nepal.

I asked Geoff if he was ok to travel by train and car to Kathmandu from Kolkata. A 17-hour train ride followed by a 150km drive. Geoff readily agreed. Little did I know he had mentally translated the 150km drive to a 1.5 – 2-hour duration!

by Baishakhi Connor

Ah the perils of unfamiliar language and assumptions. Himalayan winding roads with an old Nepalese car meant the 150km usually took 6 hours. A truck accident shut the narrow path, adding an extra 3 hours to our journey.

We still laugh about Geoff's assumption and his repeated "Are we there yet?" through the bumpy car ride.

I came back from the holiday with new energy. I redoubled my job search efforts, refining my approach and seeking out new opportunities with a new sense of purpose. And I had energy for more.

One weekend in October I saw an ad in the local paper advertising a fun run near home. On a whim, I joined. I hadn't run since school. In fact, I did not even have appropriate clothes and wore jeans and t-shirt! Attempting a 5km run, I nearly passed out at the 100m mark!

I walked and shuffled the rest of the way to finish in under an hour. However, this triggered a new goal. I would run. I would get fit. In November, I joined a running group. I left home at 4:30am three times a week to run. It took me two years, but I eventually finished a half marathon, running the entire way without stopping!

In November, my interviews also started to pick up. The break in India and the activities I had been up to filled me with confidence and I felt good. I learnt to take rejections in my stride, and even made some lasting connections from jobs I didn't get. As summer rolled in, I interviewed with a consulting firm and knew I had smashed it. Even then, the call for the second round with their partner felt surreal, almost dreamlike.

by Baishakhi Connor

Yet I knew not to pin my hopes on it.
At the final interview, they offered me a position more senior than the one I had applied for. I was to join on 1 February, leaving me another 6 weeks of summer to enjoy without the gnawing anxiety of unemployment.

The elation was unlike anything I had felt before. After twelve long months of uncertainty and perseverance, I had finally secured my first job in Australia. The summer sun on my face felt like nature's spotlight on me, a personal celebration.

The family Christmas that year was special. Sit down lunch and dinner for nearly a 100 people, all family. This was no mean feat. I felt welcome, I belonged. Geoff's parents, siblings and I booked a week away together. We went on beach walks, had dinners together, and made many memories.

In January, the last month before I would go back to work, Geoff and I took all the kids away to a seaside resort in Coff's Harbour. Geoff and I drove for 17 hours, the kids flew in. It was the last time they would all come away with us together, and without their own partners and kids. We spent hours in the pool and the beaches and went on mini hikes.

But the enduring memory is our first skydiving experience.
I don't remember who suggested it first. But soon we found ourselves lined up as a family, learning how to jump out of a perfectly good plane.

When our little plane reached 15,000ft, the door opened, and Geoff went first with his instructor. I watched him leap into the void and instantly become a speck in the sky.

It was my turn. I felt a rush of nerves and an overwhelming sense of excitement. Strapped securely to my tandem instructor, I took a deep breath and jumped.

by Baishakhi Connor

To my surprise, I didn't feel the stomach-dropping sensation of a roller coaster. The ground was so far below, it felt like we were flying above a distant landscape that drifted slowly under us.

As we fell freely through the air, there was a powerful rush of wind and the exhilarating feeling of total freedom as I left complete control to my tandem instructor, trusting him entirely.

Then, the parachute deployed. We transitioned from the thrill of freefall to a serene, gliding descent. We floated, swaying gently, with a breathtaking view of the sapphire water and gold beaches beneath us. It was peaceful, almost meditative.

In that moment, I reflected on the past year—a year of immense challenges and growth. I had to fight hard to find a new job in a new country, adapt as a new immigrant, navigate my role as a new wife, and bond as a new stepmother. Through it all, I learned to find my footing and carve out a place for myself in a new world. I had learned to let go, to embrace life without trying to control every outcome. I had discovered that joy could be found in the unpredictable, the uncontrollable, and the effort itself.

Floating gently through the air, I felt an overwhelming sense of accomplishment and pure, unadulterated joy.
I had finally found my place.

"I hear people describing their lives as a tapestry or patchwork quilt. I remember thinking mine resembles the ancient Japanese art of Kintsugi – where broken pottery is made whole again with the pieces held together by gold, silver or platinum."

Judith Jordan

I studied a Bachelor of Laws and Bachelor of Arts Degree at the University of Adelaide, obtained my Graduate Diploma of Legal Practice from the University of South Australia and was admitted to practice in 1998.

Post-admission, I worked at the Legal Services Commission of South Australia, then in private practice with two well-respected law firms. I was one of the first solicitors trained in Collaborative Practice and worked to establish it nationally, becoming a founding member of the Australian Academy of Collaborative Practitioners. I have been in sole practice since 2009 and proudly badged my firm as being alternative dispute resolution focused. Being a Nationally Accredited Mediator and a Parenting Coordinator, my focus, where children are concerned, is to bring parents together to develop their unique parenting style to cater for the dynamics of their family as their children transition between two supportive households.

ABOUT THE AUTHOR

In property matters, I work with clients to delve into their fears over their financial situation and what may or may not happen and focus on the future by working towards a just and equitable settlement that takes their future needs and past contribution into account.

I am the founding member of ResolutionSA, which is a group of solicitors and allied professionals who work to assist clients to reach a final agreement by consent and without recourse to adversarial litigation.

I devote time to the Law Society of SA Small Practice Committee where I am the Acting Chair and a member of the Alternate Dispute Resolution Committee.

Away from the office, I enjoy spending time with my husband and our blended family of 5 children, 5 grandchildren and exhibiting and caring for our cats. For my sins I am also the President of the Australian Cat Federation of Australia which probably came about because they needed a new Constitution!

Website	judithjordan.com.au
Facebook	/JudithJordanLawyer.
Linkedin	/judith-jordan

A repurposed life

On the way home, my partner phoned and told me I had to come back to Paediatric Intensive Care at the hospital. Whatever this thing was had moved and our son had to be resuscitated. He was on life support. I walked into a very surreal scene. Our two-year-old son was lit up like a Christmas tree...

In early 2001, I was sent by my firm down to an old Courtroom at the Supreme Court to receive judgment. I had to be fully robed. It was a quite warm day and the air-conditioning was renowned for not working. As I sat at the bar table I started to feel unwell. While trying to work out why I felt unwell I had cause to look in my diary and it dawned on me that I was late. Women reading this will understand what that means. Once judgment was delivered and the court adjourned, I strode out as quickly as I could, ripping off my wig, jabot and gown, certain I was going to vomit at any moment, and made my way to the fresh air of the street. I saw my GP later that day and the good conservative Catholic man that he was, told me that it was too early to do a pregnancy test and in any event wasn't it wonderful that I was in a lovely stable relationship. I wanted to hit him.

The next day I did a pregnancy test during my lunchbreak – it was positive. That evening, I drove towards my partner's home crying all the way. This wasn't in the plan.

by Judith Jordan

My partner had been in a car accident and was suffering from whiplash when I burst in and blubbered the results of the pregnancy test. I remember looking up into this face. He was happy and calm. He reassured me that everything would be fine. In my head, I was resistant to the idea. We went on however, had the pregnancy confirmed, and made plans for how we would cope. We had been in our relationship for four years but were very sensitive to blending two families who had gone through the marriages of their parents' ending. We were taking things very slowly for their sake.

The pregnancy was not without its difficulties. It became a semi-regular occurrence on Friday afternoons for me to arrive at hospital with my work trolley and overnight bag. There I would spend weekends while my blood sugars were brought under control due to my gestational diabetes. My weekly appointments at the Medical Complications Clinic were also quite an undertaking though I can see the funny side now. With my secretary ringing the specialist's secretary to see how late he was running and me timing my arrival to coincide with most of the staff leaving the outpatient clinic and the obstetrician and I discussing wider family law issues and my pregnancy and its difficulties... it was a coordination nightmare!

On 8 October 2001, I went into labour about 1:30pm, shortly before I had several client appointments. The only person in the office who knew I was in labour was my secretary, Mary. We made it through the afternoon then I drove to Adelaide for the combined office weekly meeting. We then adjourned to the pub around the corner for some socialising and eventually I looked at my watch and announced to my 3 male colleagues that the contractions were now 15 minutes apart and I'd better start heading for home.

by Judith Jordan

I drove to my mother's, had a rest, then drove to my partner's home as we had been living together for a few months.

At about 2:30 am, we headed to the hospital. I would just like to say that whoever thought it was a good idea to put speed humps near the entry to Emergency at that hospital, is on my hit list!

Our son was born a little after 8am.

Paid maternity leave didn't exist in October 2001 and I was extremely lucky to have wonderful employers who allowed me to use accumulated sick leave, holiday pay and 'yet to accumulate' sick leave and holiday pay to have 6 weeks at home with our new son.

I returned to work complete with a breast pump and a baby poo brown Décor 2 bottle wine cooler to transport the small bottles of milk to and from the office. My colleagues had to take care in the bar fridge when assessing milk choices for their tea and coffee.

Our son was a relaxed, easy-going baby and took after his father who delayed his final year and a half of his Arts and Law Degree to become a house dad before the TV show became popular.

Fast forward to January 2003 and our beautiful son started to have a series of respiratory infections. We found ourselves at the doctors commencing at one visit per week with antibiotics prescribed. By July that year, our son was sleeping beside our bed because he was snoring and needed attention throughout the night.

by Judith Jordan

The GP pointedly refused to give us a referral to an ear, nose & throat specialist (ENT).

In July 2003, I took leave from work thinking that if I was at home I could sort this out. During a vacation swimming course in the pool, I noticed that our son had something coming down his left nostril but then going up again. The swimming instructor noticed it as well and I took him home. The object came out and we sent it via the GP's room for pathology.

Two days later we met with the GP who weighed him and agreed that he had lost weight. He described the pathology as "normal nasal flora". I didn't buy that for one second.

I demanded a referral to an ENT specialist and was given the GP's usual speech. I was insistent. She instead referred us to the Sleep Disorder Clinic of the local Children's Hospital. Over the weekend, I found a new GP leading to an appointment with an ENT specialist 12 days later.

Our son's condition worsened in that time to the point where his snoring turned into choking. We sat him up several times a night before his breathing settled and he could go back to sleep. The following Friday night, his breathing worsened and we took him to hospital. He was going blue around his mouth. I knew this meant a lack of oxygen and his condition had gone to an even more serious stage.

We met with a lovely Irish resident doctor who agreed there was something serious going on. Despite investigations, no cause was identified. We left with a recommendation to use a U-shaped pillow and dread.

Next, we attended the clinic around the corner from the Children's Hospital and a full examination was undertaken.

by Judith Jordan

As the specialist got our son to say "ah" and he moved his head around I caught the look on his face as he came up. Fear stabbed me.

He told us that there were four things this could be. The last one was a Rhabdomyosarcoma. I knew sarcoma was cancer. He told us we could wait until the next day, but he preferred we walk around the corner immediately and he would have a doctor meet us at Day of Surgery Admission (DOSA). Our toddler needed a CT scan.

I left our youngster with his father to undergo the scan. I had a client appointment with someone who did not have a mobile phone, and we could not contact to cancel...

On the way home, my partner phoned and told me I had to come back to Paediatric Intensive Care at the hospital. Whatever this thing was had moved and our son had to be resuscitated. He was on life support. I walked into a very surreal scene. Our two-year-old son was lit up like a Christmas tree.

Our boy was intubated, had oxygen and various IV lines in and nothing looked normal. I spent that night for the first of many in a recliner-style chair as machines kept our son alive. I sent his father home to get what sleep he could in a bed.

Our paediatric cancer journey had begun.
Three days later we obtained a diagnosis and discussed treatment protocols. I remember looking at the young doctor giving me this choice and saying, "If this was your child, what would you do?" We followed his advice.

From early August 2003 to late March 2004, our son received nine rounds of chemotherapy. Additionally, he had over 30 radiation treatments.

by Judith Jordan

I remember when we were told about the treatment protocol, I thought I heard, "And after nine weeks he will commence daily treatments of radiotherapy." I hadn't understood that the chemotherapy would also continue. I would collect the boys from the hospital and drive them to the adult hospital. Our youngster went from a child who walked into the adult hospital in the morning relatively happy, bald as a badger with a nasogastric feeding tube pinned over the top of his head, looking a little like Rudolph the Red Nosed Reindeer because of all the tape on his nose, who was friendly and helped the adult radiotherapy patients with their jigsaw puzzles, to a child we had to carry in because he was so ill. The compassionate gazes of the adults who watched this deterioration while being on their own cancer treatment remains with me.

I hear people describing their lives as a tapestry or patchwork quilt. I remember thinking mine resembles the ancient Japanese art of Kintsugi – where broken pottery is made whole again with the pieces held together by gold, silver or platinum. We had the pieces, the treatment was the precious metal.

As the treatment progressed radiation burns emerged on his face. You would see skin on his face burning bright red after each treatment and eventually it began to weep. We were instructed by the radiologists to put Sorbolene cream on it which I felt made it worse holding the heat in. I did some research and found an Australian made gel that was developed for the burns' victims of the Bali Bombing. I sought permission to apply that instead. I was given permission, somewhat reluctantly, and we would watch the red and heat fade as much as it could from his face as he was recovering from his general anaesthetic each morning. The adult patients asked what we were using – we were happy to share the information.

by Judith Jordan

However, the combination of chemotherapy and radiotherapy at the same time made him extremely ill.

Our son had loved the Christmas pageant the year before and all he wanted to do was get out of that hospital and be involved. Various doctors, nurses and his parents made the foolish promise that he would make it to the pageant. As the weeks went on, plans kept changing.

He watched the pageant on TV in a listless state from his hospital bed.

I recall poking Christmas decorations up through the ceiling tiles and blowing up an ornamental Christmas tree to try and make his room look festive. I knew he was extremely ill by his vacant stare at the screen above his bed. There was no reaction when pageant clowns came to visit. His burns were bleeding and all I did that day was deal with that. Each time I went with dirty linen into the corridor, the other mums and dads would come out of their rooms offering support.

We all knew this wasn't good.
He was assessed by the paediatric Intensive care team and taken back to intensive care.

The chemo stopped and the radiotherapy stopped, and his beautiful face was allowed to heal. Treatment was complete. March 2005, in the middle of a staff gathering, my secretary announced she had the oncologist on the phone. I excused myself. When I returned, the room hushed. They looked frightened. I told them the Oncologist had called it... the cancer was officially in remission! The room erupted with people cheering, laughing and hugging me but somehow deep in my being I was not able to relax and be excited.

by Judith Jordan

In my head all I could think of was, you can't irradiate the brain of a toddler and fill his body up with drugs and suddenly it's all right.

I was right. Paediatric cancer is the 'gift' that keeps on giving. We quickly found ourselves with over eight specialists and departments that we had to regularly consult with.

Before the end of his treatment, I arranged for our son to return to kindergarten so that he didn't lose any more time with his peers as I was acutely aware he had missed out on a significant amount of the rough and tumble of early childhood where boundaries are tested, and children start to learn resilience. Instead, he had spent many months of his life connected to tubes and machines and interacting mainly with adults. The Clown Doctors and the Starlight Foundation sending Captain Starlight around were welcome respite to this, however I knew his resilience and ability to cope in a normal childhood setting had been significantly compromised. He was in and out of hospital with infections regularly for the first year following treatment.

Throughout his illness I had to keep working. My partner had to take a leave of absence from his study because one of us had to earn the money and the other had to be the on-call parent, otherwise we simply would not financially have survived. There is a huge financial cost to the families of not only childhood cancer patients but any child who suffers a disability or a significant illness. Charities are very helpful and do what they can, but mortgages and bills still must be paid.

I had returned to work less than a week after the initial CT scan. Some of my female work colleagues were less than helpful and in fact criticised me for working.

by Judith Jordan

In general though, my personal assistant and the staff in general at the law firm at which I worked were fabulous. I was able to come and go as I needed. I was successful because of support given by friends and colleagues who believed in me.

I sometimes say that my bullshit meter has been full since around August 2003. That diagnosis rearranged what was important in life.

I recall during this time having a client who was arguing with their ex-spouse over two garden pots. They both wanted them. I pondered the value of the pots versus the costs of the argument and wondered if letting them go might be better value. The client let them go. This is just one example of how learning not to sweat the small stuff helped me to become a better family lawyer.

I recall during this time having a client who was arguing with their ex-spouse over two garden pots. They both wanted them.

I pondered the value of the pots versus the costs of the argument and wondered if letting them go might be better value. The client let them go. This is just one example of how learning not to sweat the small stuff helped me to become a better family lawyer.

Our boy went to school with his peers, and we had more medical issues arise. The purpose of this story is that whilst a diagnosis of childhood cancer is something that I would never wish on my worst enemy, it has made all of us in our family better people. Our youngest son is a wonderful empathetic and sensitive young man who reaches out to the underdog.

by Judith Jordan

He has this innate ability to sense when someone needs a helping hand, and I have recently seen that when sadly one of his friends was murdered, the care he took of his friends during that very sad time. He knew which of the circle of friends would struggle and he reached out to them and gathered them all in to ensure no one was left behind.

Had our family not had that diagnosis and undertaken that cancer journey, I don't think I would have acquired the skillset that enables me to be the sounding board, the naïve empathetic inquisitive inquirer who poses the questions to help people reflect and reach within themselves and find their answers with support and move forward.

Like the ancient Japanese art of Kintsugi, I am the vessel that is together again, but I recognise the beauty that has come, despite the initial damage.

We live a new normal post our paediatric cancer journey, but like a piece of Kintsugi, it is a beautiful one enhanced by the medical, nursing and other staff brought into our lives and the deep bonds of understanding with fellow parents and children on the same journey and our friends who journeyed with us.

"It's an emotional rollercoaster full of excitement and anxiety, loneliness and discovery. Embrace the challenge with an open mind and heart and you might find it becomes the experience of a lifetime."

Stephanie Lee

Join Stephanie on a transformative journey through relocation as she combines her extensive corporate background with her roles as an emerging author and successful entrepreneur. As the co-founder and director of Quest Data Link Sdn Bhd and Branch Director for Business In Heels in Malaysia, Stephanie is dedicated to helping professional and businesswomen recognize and articulate their value, make a meaningful impact, and achieve the rewards they deserve. With over twenty-six years of experience across IT, financial services, and payments, Stephanie's career has taken her from her hometown of Ipoh to dynamic cities like Singapore, Kuala Lumpur, and Hong Kong. In her engaging book, she offers personal anecdotes from these relocations, illustrating how each move has profoundly influenced her growth and enriched her life.

ABOUT THE AUTHOR

Stephanie's narrative is a tribute to women navigating the complexities of relocating for personal and professional growth. She candidly explores her triumphs and setbacks, the risks she faced, and the invaluable lessons learned. Her story highlights the challenges and rewards of finding a sense of home in new cities, emphasizing resilience and adaptability.

Relocating can be both exhilarating and daunting, a rollercoaster of excitement and anxiety, loneliness and self-discovery. Stephanie's reflections highlight how each move has been a lesson in embracing change and pursuing personal fulfilment. Her story offers a beacon of inspiration for anyone contemplating a major relocation or seeking purpose through change.

Stephanie's experiences provide valuable insights for those facing the challenges of moving to a new city, offering guidance on how to turn the daunting into the rewarding. Embrace the adventure with an open heart and mind and discover how relocation can be one of the most enriching experiences of your life.

Instagram	stephanieleelyl
Facebook	/stephanie.lee
Linkedin	/stephanieyllee

Embracing change in a new city

On a sweltering afternoon in downtown Kuala Lumpur, stuck in a gruelling traffic jam after a taxing client meeting, I felt both drained and disheartened. Just then, my phone rang, jolting me from my fatigue. It was my global head.

"Drop everything," he said, urgency lacing his voice. "We need you in Hong Kong for a major opportunity."

My heart pounded with a mix of exhilaration and trepidation. The thought of a new challenge was intoxicating, yet the timing felt overwhelming.

Moving to a new environment is a daunting yet exhilarating journey we all experience. Whether it's across town or across the world, questions, concerns and fears arise making the transition delicate to process and difficult to endure. I want to share my personal story, not from a place of expertise, but from the raw, emotional perspective of someone who has navigated the highs and lows of relocation.

In my early twenties, I embarked on a brave journey from my beloved hometown of Ipoh, Malaysia to Singapore, for an engineering traineeship.

by Stephanie Lee

Saying goodbye to the familiar comforts of home was hard, but the dream of following in my uncle's footsteps and making my mark in the engineering world drove me forward. Singapore, with its mix of familiarity and newness, was both intimidating and thrilling. The city echoed with the cultural similarities of Ipoh, thanks to our shared historical and geographical ties, yet it also unveiled its own distinct identity, shaped by its unique history and demographics.

Over the course of four transformative years, Singapore became more than just a new city, it became a crucible for my personal growth. I chose to advance my education in computer science while balancing it with my work life. Juggling these demands was no simple task. Yet, this journey went beyond just career ambition, it was a confrontation between my youthful dreams and the realities of life, an intimate exploration of who I am and what I aspire to be. Every challenge I faced and every victory I achieved became a crucial step in uncovering my true self.

Four years later, in my late twenties, I made another bold move and left Singapore to start anew in Kuala Lumpur. Without a job lined up, I was driven by a strong determination to transition my life. This wasn't just a career change; it was an opportunity to start from scratch and dive into the thriving field of information technology. It was also a chance to build a life with my boyfriend, who would soon become my spouse. The move was filled with hope and anticipation, combining the excitement of professional growth in a new field with the promise of a shared future. Our son was born in this multi-cultural city, bringing a new depth of joy into our lives. I had the chance to shape my family life, home, and an IT career in Kuala Lumpur.

by Stephanie Lee

In later years, three of my siblings moved closer to me to pursue their education and build their own careers and families. The challenges and successes along the way made this journey deeply rewarding and fulfilling.

In my late forties, I found myself trapped in a comfort zone that had begun to feel stifling. My career had reached a plateau where my expertise was recognized, but the routine had become monotonous. On a sweltering afternoon in downtown Kuala Lumpur, stuck in a gruelling traffic jam after a taxing client meeting, I felt both drained and disheartened. Just then, my phone rang, jolting me from my fatigue. It was my global head.

"Drop everything," he said, urgency lacing his voice. "We need you in Hong Kong for a major opportunity."

My heart pounded with a mix of exhilaration and trepidation. The thought of a new challenge was intoxicating, yet the timing felt overwhelming. At this stage in my life, relocating wasn't as simple as it once was. Unlike the past when I could easily pick up and go, this time I had a family to consider.

After some discussions with my family, their encouragement and unwavering support helped me see the opportunity through a new lens. The timing seemed almost serendipitous, my son was preparing to leave home for college, which might make the transition smoother, but my spouse would need to stay behind due to his business commitments.

With a heart full of both excitement and anxiety, I boarded the plane to Hong Kong. The promotion was a significant leap forward in my career, and I spent the next three and a half

by Stephanie Lee

years immersing myself in this fulfilling new role. The transition was far from easy, but the steadfast support from my loved ones and the promise of a new chapter made every challenge worthwhile.

When choosing a new city to move, the stakes are significant. You'll need to consider job opportunities, lifestyle, climate, and cost of living. Additionally, it's crucial to mentally prepare for the transition. Embrace the excitement of a fresh start and imagine how you can thrive in your new surroundings.

When I faced the choice between Singapore and Hong Kong, Singapore felt familiar, but Hong Kong's vibrant, dynamic appeal drew me in. I was eager for a new challenge and a chance to experience a different culture. My background in Malaysia, with its rich cultural diversity, made me confident in adapting to Hong Kong's unique blend of Eastern and Western influences. I was eager to explore Hong Kong's culture more deeply, inspired by my previous work and holiday short visits, and my fondness for Cantonese films from my youth.

The humid subtropical climate, hot summers and mild winters was just one aspect.

However, what I focused on were the city's opportunities, which promised to advance my career and boost my earnings. Though the cost of living is high, it's manageable for a single person compared to a family.

I weighed the cost of living, tax system, visa requirements, and Hong Kong's competitive edge. The city's status as a financial hub and gateway to global markets was irresistible. Securing a working visa was simple with my employer's help.

by Stephanie Lee

Reports and statistics provided a broad overview, but it was the conversations with future colleagues and HR that truly revealed what life in Hong Kong would be like. Speaking directly with people offered an invaluable, authentic perspective of the city. Ultimately, my decision was about seizing career opportunities and immersing myself in a city with a distinct rhythm and vibrant energy.

No matter how much you plan or research, nothing can quite compare to the moment you step into your new city. The thrill of experiencing new streets, people, and buildings firsthand is an adventure that no guidebook can prepare you for. I vividly remember my arrival in Hong Kong with just two suitcases. The city's vibrant energy was palpable, but navigating this new world required a bit more than excitement.

To start settling in, the first step is finding temporary housing. I arranged a one-month stay at Sharma, a serviced apartment chain near my workplace. This gave me the opportunity to explore and adjust to the city. It's a wise strategy, allowing me to find a place that truly suited me as it gave me the immediate convenience of a no-fuss, furnished and serviced apartment.

Hong Kong's dazzling skyscrapers contrast sharply with the modest conditions many locals live in. Finding affordable housing can be a real challenge due to high land prices and intense competition. Engaging a seasoned real estate agent is crucial when scouting for a long-term lease. They offer insights into rental budgets, local amenities, schools, and the community making the whole experience less overwhelming. After a month of searching, I secured a cozy 500-square-foot apartment in Wan Chai. It's central and convenient. It became home.

by Stephanie Lee

At first, the city's rapid pace and cultural quirks were both exhilarating and daunting. The bustling streets, constant buzz of activity, and unique cultural habits felt like a whirlwind. I often compared it to the more relaxed atmosphere of home. However, I quickly came to appreciate Hong Kong's efficient public transportation, like the MTR and the double-decker trams, especially in contrast to the traffic jams I was accustomed to.

Despite the high cost of living, exploring beyond the flashy business districts revealed more budget-friendly shopping and dining options. If high-end malls aren't your style, there are plenty of lively markets to explore. Hong Kong's vibrant culinary scene, which combines Chinese and Western influences, was easier to navigate and adapt, thanks to my familiarity with Cantonese cuisine.

While Cantonese is the main language, English is commonly used in business and on street signs, making it easier to get around. Knowing basic Cantonese phrases also helps when ordering food or shopping locally.

Learning to accept the differences and taking time to adapt turned my initial challenges into a rewarding adventure.

Adjusting to a new city like Hong Kong is a journey of both adaptation and discovery. During this period, I worked hard to establish a routine that balanced work with leisure. This new pattern incorporated gym sessions, hiking and exploring the city and it became my anchor, providing stability amidst the whirlwind of change. I'm sure it's perfectly normal for it to take weeks or months to settle into a routine that feels right. It did for me.

by Stephanie Lee

I was fortunate that one of my old friends from Malaysia had already relocated to Hong Kong years ago. Her and her family's companionship served as an anchor, helping me establish my footing in the new city for which I was truly grateful.

Making new connections, however, proved more challenging. In a city where social bonds can feel like a steep hill to climb, I learned that friendships don't form overnight. Initially, I found camaraderie among work colleagues, transforming casual after-work drinks into genuine friendships. I also joined local clubs and organizations, such as the Malaysian Chamber of Commerce, which provided both social and professional networking opportunities.

From my experience, not every encounter will result in deep connections, and that's perfectly fine. The important thing was to stay persistent and consistently show up at work, the gym, or social events. Each interaction, no matter how minor, helped me get closer to finding my place in the new city. Websites like Meetup.com helped me discover interest-based groups, making it easier to engage with others. As a first timer, stepping into a room full of strangers was intimidating.

Bringing a friend along helped ease the discomfort. Despite the anxiety, every step I venture outside my comfort zone brought me the self-improvement I craved.

Three months into my move, the excitement of the new adventure began to wane and I was left grappling with loneliness, homesickness, and mounting anxiety. My once thrilling change now felt overwhelming. Insomnia and loss of appetite became my unwanted companions and the smallest tasks becoming daunting.

by Stephanie Lee

I yearned for the comfort of my family and the familiarity of life back home.

To overcome these disheartening feelings, I focused on personalizing my new space. I decorated with touches that mattered to me by choosing my favourite sofa, equipping my kitchen, adding fresh flowers and plants, and surrounding myself with familiar comforts. Eventually, my sanctuary of solace and familiarity comforted me and helped ease me through a trying time.

This is how I'm wired. I've learned that finding a sense of home in a new city extends beyond unpacking and exploring unfamiliar streets. It's about creating a space where I feel safe and comfortable. This emotional connection is essential for my well-being and mental health. It's not just about the physical environment but also about integrating into a new routine, embracing the local culture, and building relationships that make me feel grounded.

Finding a sense of home often involved reaching out to new people and reconnecting with old friends to share joyful moments. It didn't follow a set timeline. Some may adapt quickly, others take more time.

For me, it took six months to establish a routine and truly feel at home. Patience and positivity were crucial, as building new habits and connections took time. Embracing the journey with an open heart made each step easier.

Staying connected with loved ones back home through FaceTime and WhatsApp became a vital lifeline.

by Stephanie Lee

Their visits and my trips back to Malaysia provided moments of joy and connection that eased the distance, helping me feel less lonely, more stable.

By the sixth month, things began to change. My routine solidified, I felt more at ease with my new life, made new friends, and managed my homesickness better. While the transition was challenging, these small victories made a significant difference, and I started to feel at home.

One of the most important lessons I learned was to face culture disorientation with an open heart and a willingness to embrace the unexpected. I took my time, allowing myself the freedom to explore and not pushing too hard. Gradually, I began saying yes to invitations, savouring unfamiliar foods, and diving into the rich array of new experiences that Hong Kong had to offer.

For instance, my daily commute from Wan Chai to Times Square at Causeway Bay often involves taking the tram. I get off under the Canal Road Flyover, also known to locals as Goose Neck Bridge, and walk the rest of the way to Times Square. Along the way, I see elderly women sitting on small stools surrounded by red boxes and joss-sticks, beating effigies of white tigers, a fascinating tradition, especially vibrant during the Ching Che festival.

Weekends turned into my personal adventures by hiking trails like the Victoria Peak Loop. On workdays, I concentrated on quick workouts at the Bowen Road trail, conveniently located right across from my home.

by Stephanie Lee

I also enjoyed the scenic bus rides to Stanley Main Beach, where I could relax with a coffee after a satisfying lunch at one of the restaurants at Stanley. The bus ride offered stunning views, from skyscrapers to the shores of Deep Water and Repulse Bays, scenes I will cherish for a lifetime.

Another scenic experience I particularly enjoyed after work on Friday evenings was taking the ferry rides from Wan Chai to Tsim Sha Tsui. It offered a stunning view of Hong Kong's skyline and Victoria Harbour at sunset.

Meeting friends for lunch at the Kowloon Cricket Club became a regular treat. Sometimes my friend would drive us to Sai Kung for fresh seafood dinners, adding extra joy to my weekends. I immersed myself in new activities I never imagined I would. Whether it was preparing for the Dragon Boat competition as part of a work team-building event or enthusiastically cheering at the annual Rugby Sevens... I threw myself in.

Embracing experiences and integrating into the local culture eased my homesickness and helped me settle into my new life. Each adventure brought me closer to feeling at home in Hong Kong. Whether you're adjusting quickly or gradually, navigating cultural disorientation is part of the process. Establishing a supportive network and focusing on long-term goals, career development and personal growth can help you find a sense of belonging in a new city.

Due to my relocation experience, I assisted a colleague who moved from London to Hong Kong. It was lovely to be part of someone else's successful transition.

by Stephanie Lee

Moving to a new city on your own is undeniably tough. Reflecting on my journey, each move has been a profound lesson in resilience and adaptability. It's an emotional rollercoaster full of excitement and anxiety, loneliness and discovery. Embrace the challenge with an open mind and heart and you might find it becomes the experience of a lifetime.

Returning home after living abroad can be just as challenging as you navigate reverse culture shock and the changes that have occurred in your absence. Your old routines and familiar places might seem different, and you may struggle with the sense that you no longer fit in. This can be disheartening as you adjust to changes in your family, friends, and even in the rhythm of your own home. It's like starting the adjustment process all over again, but with the wisdom gained from your experiences, you can adjust and find your place once more.

Whether you're moving for a new job, a change in environment, or personal reasons, consider your feelings and motivations carefully. Relocation can be a chance for a fresh start, new opportunities, and personal growth. Though the transition can be tough, embracing the journey and staying open to change will lead you to new joys and discoveries.

Other books in the series

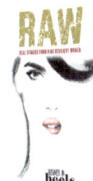

RAW ~ Real Stories from Nine Resilient Women

Shame, Guilt, Ridicule, Poverty, Horror, Impotence, Violence, Fear. Nevertheless, it seems we get an (un) healthy dose of those sometimes too. Mostly, it's not a case of if… it's when. And while you can surround yourself with positive and like-minded people to help you through, when all is said and done, it's those lonely hours between 2am and 4am when we often find ourselves facing our demons.

RAW explores the trials of nine everyday women who chose to carry on. Sure, there's some baggage… but that's a hell of a lot healthier than being continuously beaten up by those demons. Feeling like it's all about you? It's not. Take comfort from the stories of others who've walked a few miles on some windy, rocky roads through their own barren wastelands…and emerged stronger, sharper and ready to get on with it.

Need a new perspective? RAW may help set you on a happier path.

Get your copy now businessinheels.net/raw-book

Business in Heels' books

Rise Above ~ beyond ordinary

This collection of stories show the might and power of eight women who refuse to be beaten. Together, they have endured hardship, broken marriages, health crises, catastrophes, self-doubt, parental discouragement, business failure and more.

Yet with grit and determination and fire in their bellies, they have forged on and rebuit their lives, businesses and careers. Their courage, resilience and deep sense of purpose has enabled each to find her path.

Get your copy now businessinheels.net/riseabove-book-order

Business in Heels' books

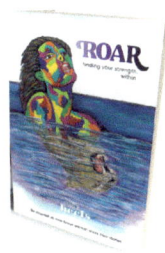

Roar ~ finding your strength, within.

These nine courageous women have gone out of their way to tell it like it is. Prepare to be shocked, to cry, to admire their bravery. Prepare to shake your head in disbelief.

Whatever your reaction, know that these women are no longer prepared to cork it, sit still and look pretty. Prepare to hear them... *Roar!*

Get your copy now businessinheels.net/roarbook

Renewal ~ Real stories, real advice from eleven remarkable women

Life throws curve balls at us all.

Some we see coming so we duck and weave in time to avoid them. Others hit us smack in the face and leave a lasting scar. Others we see collide with loved ones and we're paralysed by the ricochet.

There is no single path life's lessons take to us, no orbit you can sail to avoid them and no chance they will ever arrive at a good time. The only guarantee is that life will send the experiences and it's up to us to learn from them.

Moreover, the generous among us will share their lessons so others may avoid their pain.

This is the story of... *Renewal*

Get your copy now businessinheels.net/renewal-book

Business in Heels' books

Inspire ~ A life of purpose

Embark on an exhilarating journey through the lives of seven brave women who've fearlessly shattered boundaries and embraced their unique purposes. These powerful stories from a trailblazing fisherwoman, an emergency services responder, to a determined single mother turned entrepreneur, exude resilience and authenticity. "Inspire: A Life of Purpose" is a heartfelt homage to womanhood and the unwavering human spirit, leaving you uplifted and forever transformed.

Get your copy now — businessinheels.net/inspire-book

www.ingramcontent.com/pod-product-compliance
Lightning Source LLC
Chambersburg PA
CBHW042047290426
44109CB00006B/139